ONCE & FOREVER

b

Once & Forever

The Story of Mount Airy Granite
A Revision

By Karen Jones Hall

Copyright 2012 by Karen Jones Hall

Once & Forever

(c) October 2012

ISBN-13: 978-1482523362
ISBN-10: 1482523361

All rights reserved. Except for use in any review, the reproduction or utilization of this work in whole or in part in any form by any electronic, mechanical, or other means, now known or hereafter invented, including photocopying or recording, or in any information storage or retrieval system, is forbidden without the written permission of the author, Karen J. Hall, 3802 Laurel Forest Ct., Colfax, NC 27235.

WELCOME TO THE
NORTH CAROLINA GRANITE CORPORATION
"WORLD'S LARGEST OPEN-FACE GRANITE QUARRY"

Other works by Karen Hall with Arcadia Publishing:

Wythe County, Virginia, Images of America Series

The Blue Ridge Parkway, the Vintage Postcard Series

Building the Blue Ridge Parkway, Images of America Series

Guilford Battleground Military Park Monuments

Contents

Dedication..i
Photo Credits...ii
Prologue..iii
Chapter 1........History of the Quarry......................................1
Chapter 2........Cape Fear & Yadkin Valley Railroad............21
Chapter 3........John Davis "Jack" Sargent..........................31
Chapter 4........Master Stonecutters......................................33
Chapter 5........Harry Barton, Architect................................47
Chapter 6........Tesh Construction...53
Chapter 7........Granite Buildings in Mount Airy.................57
Chapter 8........Granite Mausoleums.....................................77
Chapter 9........Granite Churches..105
Chapter 10......Granite Homes...125
Chapter 11......Granite Bridges...171
Chapter 12......Granite Monuments....................................175
Chapter 13......Green Hill Cemetery...................................199
Chapter 14......NC State Bell Tower...................................205
Chapter 15......Guilford Battle Ground..............................211
Chapter 16......Kress Department Stores...........................229
Chapter 17......Granite Courthouses..................................233
Chapter 18......Mount Airy Granite Overlook...................245
Chapter 19......More Granite Buildings..............................247
Chapter 20......FDR Four Freedoms Park..........................259
Granite Humor..266
Timeline..267
Bibliography..269
Web Pages..270
Index...271

e

Dedication

In memory and honor of all of the great stonemasons that have carved into the Mount Airy Granite, I dedicate this book.

In remembrance of those that have lost their lives carving into the granite, I, also dedicate this book. I not only love the stone but the artwork that they created.

North Carolina Granite Employees sitting next to the rails waiting to load granite standing behind them. – Courtesy of the Surry County Historical Society

A Big Thank You!

    First let me thank my new group, The Blue Ridge Authors, for your undying support and encouragement. Thank you for going along with my ideas. It has been a blast. Donna thank you for my beautiful cover.
    Second, I offer a very sincere thank you to my editor and friend, Debbie Hall. You have made this a better book with your eye for detail and for that I am grateful.
    Last but not least, I thank my family, Clint, Kate, Greg, Mom, Dad, Ruby, Paul, and everyone that has put up with me through this process. Thank you for having faith in me.
    I would like to thank the Surry County Historical Society for preserving the wonderful rich history of Surry County and the photos of the North Carolina Granite Quarry.

Photo Credits

Photos courtesy of the Mount Airy Museum of Regional History, Surry County Historical Society including the Ruth Minick Collection, and from the personal collection of the author.

This fabulous photo has nine stonecutters standing on a cutout of granite circa 1900. Courtesy of the Surry County Historical Society, Minick Collection.

Prologue

The finest building material in America was discovered in Mount Airy, North Carolina many years ago. It was so long ago that the Moravians of Bethabara and Salem sent elders to chisel enough granite to carve grist mill stones from the granite. No one knows but we could speculate that it took more than one team of horses to haul the granite from Mount Airy to Salem.

Once discovered, master businessmen organized a company that created high quality stone projects. Artistic projects screamed to the world that they were created by the masters. Today those talented artists are all but forgotten.

Located in the foothills of the Blue Ridge Mountains is the largest open faced granite quarry in the world. Astronauts can see if from the heavens above the earth. Until the late nineteenth century, the value of this large "Flat Rock" was undervalued. It took the entrepreneurial skills of Thomas Woodroffe to really explore the many uses of the granite and Jack Sargent to market the product during the Roaring 30's.

On February 25, 1885, the city of Mount Airy incorporated. Main Street was bustling with business, the railroad was on the way, and people were swarming to Mount Airy to live, work, and vacation. Once it became a permanent stop on the railroad, traveling stonecutters would hop a rail car and travel to Mount Airy in search of work at the granite quarry.

From this "Rock" have came many nicknames for the small town of Mount Airy. Aside from being Andy Griffith's home place and the fictional town of Mayberry, it is also known as "The Granite City," "Flat Rock," and the new current nickname is "The Friendliest City," and that stands very true.

Mount Airy Granite can be found all over the world but most notably in North Carolina, Virginia, and Pennsylvania. A definite connection between the cities of Mount Airy and Greensboro, North Carolina was established once the railroad came into Mount Airy. A tour of Oakdale Cemetery in Mount Airy and Green Hill Cemetery Greensboro will, also, connect the two cities through businessmen. Mount Airy Granite at one time was definitely the stone of choice for many.

We can say that the State of North Carolina has been blessed with an abundant source of "the noble rock," granite. The North Carolina

Granite Corporation quarry is the largest open face granite quarry in the world measuring one mile long and 1,800 feet in width. The "noble rock" from this quarry is unblemished, gleaming, and without interfering seams to mar its splendor. Of high quality, this granite allows its widespread use as a building material, in both industrial and laboratory applications where super smooth surfaces are necessary.

North Carolina granite has been used for many magnificent edifices of government throughout the United States such as the Wright Brothers Memorial at Kitty Hawk, the gold depository at Fort Knox, the Arlington Memorial Bridge and numerous courthouses throughout the country. Mount Airy granite is a symbol of strength and steadfastness, qualities characteristic of North Carolinians. Therefore it is befitting and just that the State recognize the contribution of granite in providing employment to its citizens and enhancing the beauty of its public buildings.

Read this book and discover why North Carolina declared granite as the State Rock.

The General Assembly of 1979 designated Granite as the official Rock for the State of North Carolina. (Session Laws, 1979, c. 906). It is also a symbol of New Hampshire, Massachusetts, South Carolina, Vermont, and Wisconsin.

http://www.secretary.state.nc.us/pubsweb/symbols/sy-grani.htm

Vintage aerial photo of the North Carolina Granite Corporation quarry. Courtesy of the Surry County Historical Society Minick Collection

Mount Airy Granite Checkers Table

v

CHAPTER 1

HISTORY OF THE QUARRY

The absolute age of Mount Airy Granite is not really known. Geologically speaking it is younger than the metasedimentary schists and gneisses of the Precambrian age. In other words, it is as old as dirt. Some have predicted that it is Paleozoic, 290 million years to 590 million years old.

Size and shape wise, the mass is oval, in a general northeast-southwest direction, about 8 miles long by 4 miles wide with bedrock of about 20 to 25 square miles. It underlies the city of Mount Airy and can be seen in rock outcroppings all in the area, even in the basements of some buildings.

The color and texture is roughly uniform throughout making it a perfect building material. A building or monument can be repaired 100 years from the manufacture and expect to have the same color and quality of material.

Mount Airy Granite is very heavy. Testing shows that one cubic foot weighs 165 lbs. The crushing strength is about 29,233 pounds per square inch. Ouch!

Richard V. Dietrich, former Professor in the Department of Geological Sciences at Virginia Polytechnic Institute (Virginia Tech) studied Mount Airy Granite and wrote several pieces of literature in the 1960's about Mount Airy Granite. He established an Engineering Experiment Station at the Quarry.

During his discussion of Mount Airy "Granite" he starts off by saying that it is actually a "leucogranodiorite." It is white to a light gray and contains, but isn't limited to, magnetite, apatite, monazite, zircon, sphene, epidote, muscovite, biotite, plagioclase, microcline, quartz, myrmekite, chlorite, and calcite. he primary component of Mount Airy Granite is epidote and muscovite. Their formation can be attributed to a consolidation of aluminum rich and magnesium poor material, hydroxyl fluxed magma that was under high pressure conditions at the time of formation.

The open-faced quarry is located in the Piedmont North Carolina town of Mount Airy, Surry County, North Carolina and is called the "North Carolina Granite Corporation." At the time of Dietrich's research it was the largest open-faced quarry in North Carolina and the nation.

Astronauts can see it from outer space.

Being a chemist by trade, it is at this point that I describe "The Rock" in a more chemical description. In 1893, it was published by the North Carolina State Geologist the general characteristics. J. A. Holmes, author of the 1893 report, reported it to be 70.7 percent Silica, 16.5 percent Aluminum Oxide, 2.34 percent Iron Oxide, 0.29 percent Magnesium Oxide, almost 3 percent Calcium Oxide, 4.56 percent Sodium Oxide, and 2.45 percent Potassium Oxide.

Thus, with almost 5 percent sodium, I describe it visually as a "salt with a little pepper". Kind of like the seasoning created a few years ago called "Spepper"! Dietrich says that it is over saturated with silica giving it the white salty appearance. Also, it contains several oxidized metals including traces of Barium, Boron, Chromium, Copper, Lead, and others.

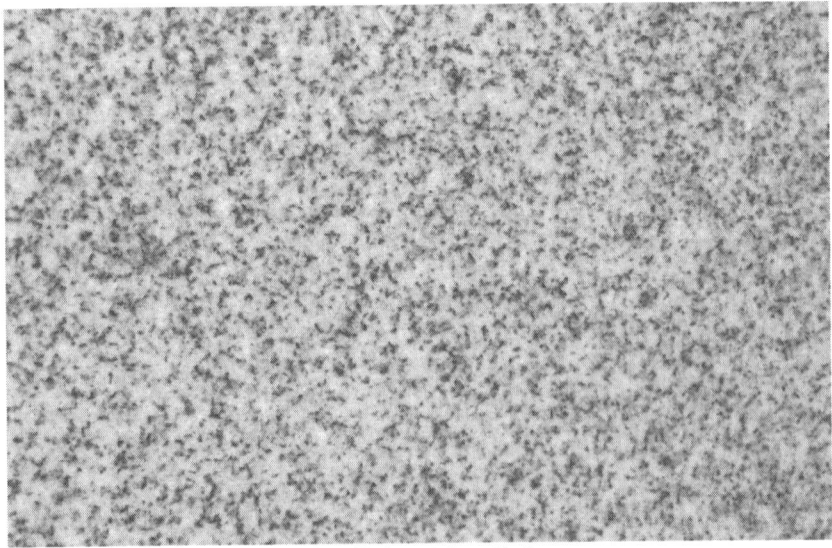

"Spepper" – Salt with a little pepper.

A modern view of the quarry.

Mining Techniques and Products

The quarry began new mining techniques in late 2000. They began a process of water jets and wire sawing in combination. This created a more efficient process by allowing more quarrying faces to be developed throughout the property and extend reserves. This created rock masses 40 feet by 40 feet. However, that is not the largest piece ever cut from the massive rock.

The saw wire is placed in vertical slots and then the granite is cut with water jets. They cut 3   inch wide slots as deep as 21 feet. The wire saw loop is placed in the slots. The floors of these sections are 40 feet by 40 feet and are cut by horizontal wire saws. Part of the machine moves backward along a track as the other part advances forward. This keeps tension on the wire not allowing for slack.

Above, this vintage photo shows a large slab of granite at the quarry. Below, Vintage postcard showing the interior of the "Shed" at the Mount Airy Granite Quarry. Courtesy of the Surry County Historical Society Minick Collection.

Above is a vintage photo showing the cutting of a very large piece of granite. Private Collection

A case tractor hauling the large piece possibly the largest ever cut. Private Collection

VIEW OF QUARRY, MT. AIRY, N. C.

This is a vintage linen postcard with cables and wires to pull the granite to the shipping yard.

Before 2000, quarrying granite used drop ball, drill, tipping boom, explosives truck and other quarrying equipment to extract the granite. It took an eye to eye or a keen eye to determine the "grain of the rock." An earlier method was based on years of experience at this rock body and was to propagate a horizontal crack eastward; done by drilling a series of closely spaced horizontal holes. Needless to say it was much more of an art form and indicative of the master mason skills that it required.

This photo was snapped sometime between 1907 and 1908 of men loading granite onto a wagon at the quarry. Courtesy of the Surry County Historical Society, Minick Collection.

Curbing

Curbing is a very common product manufactured in the shop. The blocks must be placed in the correct position because cracking will occur more easily in one direction than in another. A large hydraulic press is used to cut the curbing. Power hand tools are used to finish the process.

Curbing was used extensively in Winston-Salem during the 1920's and 1930's as can be seen in the photograph. It is ideal because the chemical treatments that are applied for ice will not harm the granite. Danville, Virginia, Washington D. C. and Raleigh, North Carolina, also, used granite curbing.

Granite curbing found in Old Salem.

Millions of school children have stepped on this chunk of granite to get a drink of water in Old Salem playing with the old well pump. Notice the granite curbing that is inlaid in the sidewalk.

This vintage postcard shows granite steps leading to Main Hall of Greensboro College sometime between 1910 and 1920.

This photo shows the same granite steps leading to Main Hall at Greensboro College in May 2011 with a new graduate, Kate E. Hall.

Ownership Timeline

Before 1524 when the first explorers came to America it would have been home to the Iroquois Indians.

In 1585, Queen Elizabeth I charted the land to Sir Walter Raleigh.

Since that colony failed, King Charles II charted it to eight Englishmen.

The quarry was first operated (on record) in 1743 by the Moravians.

In 1775, an entry in the Moravian records indicates that Brother Kapp and Brother Blum went to Mount Airy to gather Mill Stones. I am not sure who the owner was at this time, but it was quite possibly part of the Wachovia Tract of land owned by the Moravians.

In 1780, Thomas Smith, a stonecutter, purchased for 50 shillings an acre, a 400 acre tract of land which included the quarry. This is the first registered deed for the property.

In 1782, Mr. Smith sold the land to Daniel Humphries. He then sold it to Benjamin Humphries, or possibly gave it to him. Bejamin may have been his son. Benjamin then deeded the property to Samuel Dalton. From Mr. Dalton the land then went to Tyre Glenn.

In 1840, Mr. Robert Gilmer came to Mount Airy and purchased 840 acres from Tyre Glenn that contained 40 acres of "Worthless Rock."

Thomas Woodroffe from Greensboro, North Carolina, purchased the 40 acres for $5,000. He and his four sons, Thomas, Jr., George, Frank, and William, operated the quarry for several years. Mr. Woodroffe died in 1900 and the quarry was inherited by his sons.

Mr. Woodroffe, Sr. was born in Chiddingstone Kent, England on April 16, 1829. In 1872, the Woodroffe family came to America and settled first in Virginia and later in Greensboro, North Carolina. He was the husband of Mary Ann Gibb Woodroffe. She outlived him by 10 years. His sons ran the company for the next ten years before moving to West Virginia to try their hand in coal mining.

Lumber was Mr. Woodroffe's first business of expertise in Greensboro which helped him get the contract with the Cape Fear and Yadkin Valley Railway (formerly known as the Mount Airy Railway) to build the depots from Mount Airy to Greensboro. Of course the Mount Airy train depot was the only one built completely with granite. The High Point depot has the granite ashler stone half way up the outer walls.

Mr. Woodroffe's late 1800's home in Mount Airy is a great example of Victorian eclecticism. A Queen Anne - influenced tower central bay is enhanced with a wraparound porch and Italianate paneled corner posts and wood awnings over the windows. The wraparound porch is ornamented with saw work. In the rear of the home is located a chamber room that hosted many musical events sponsored by the Woodroffes. Common knowledge is that he was more interested in music than in his granite company, "Woodroffe and Sons." His son George played cello. Thomas played the viola and Frank played the violin. Sounds a bit like Williamsburg. Today the house is painted pink and still stands in front of the First Baptist Church on North Main Street. No granite appears to have been used in the construction of his home which is not surprising since their first specialty was the timber industry.

Thomas Woodroffe, Sr. passed away at the quarry in 1900. His body was transported back to Greensboro and buried in Green Hill Cemetery. He died of Brights disease (kidney disease, elevated blood pressure). His and the family tombstones are carved from Mount Airy Granite.

Mount Airy Granite Quarry Office Force. Eight men are posing in front of an office building. According to notes on the back of the picture, they are, from left to right: W. R. Simpson (?), T. Daber, Donald Rector, John Leitch (?), Mr. Tom Woodroffe, Mr. George Woodroffe, Mr. Frank Woodroffe. A second note reads:"This is from another source: Drew Martin, W. R. Simpson, J. R. Sargent, J. T. Daber, D. C. Rector, "Pop" Leileb, Geo. Woodruff, Tom Woodruff." I believe this to be Tom Woodroffe, Jr. since Mr. Woodroffe, Sr. passed away in 1900. This is a later photo courtesy of the Surry County Historical Society, Minick Collection.

Obituary from the Charlotte Observer of July 24, 1900:

"Greensboro, July 23, 1900   Mr. Thomas Woodroffe, who had been critically ill at his home in Mount Airy for several weeks, died yesterday afternoon. The remains were brought to Greensboro today and interred in Green Hill Cemetery. Mr. Woodroffe was 71 years old, and was prominently identified with the business interests of Greensboro for a number of years. He was a contractor and builder and extensive manufacturer of lumber. About two years ago, he leased the Mount Airy granite quarries, and moved his family to that place. Mr. Woodroffe was a native of England, coming to America in 1872."

Woodroffe Family plot, built with Mount Airy Granite in Green Hill Cemetery, Greensboro, NC.

The author has discovered in research that Mr. Thomas Woodroffe, Sr. was one of the first one hundred shareholders in the Guilford Battleground Company that preserved the Revolutionary battlefield and speculates that because of his business contacts was the reason he was interred in Greensboro rather than Mount Airy.

Thomas Woodroffe's grave marker in Green Hill Cemetery, Greensboro, NC.

The tombstone of Mary Ann Woodroffe located in Green Hill Cemetery, Greensboro, NC.

Vintage photo of a Case Tractor pulling a slab of granite to the finishing shed.

Important Company Details

Although, the company is commonly known as "Mount Airy Granite," it has never been officially been called "Mount Airy Granite." It was the "North Carolina Granite Corporation" as of
1904. They bought the rights to the name "Mount Airy Granite" so that no one else could use it but officially it has never existed.
In 1904 after Mr. Woodroffe's sons took charge they officially named it North Carolina Granite Corporation and filed the documents with the county courthouse.

North Carolina Granite Office Building

This beautiful office building was built around 1928. Great attention was paid to the detail work on the outside of the building. Considering the growth of the company at the time, it was very modest compared to other structures that were being built. This building is approximately 9,600 square feet.

1928 North Carolina Granite Corporation Office Building.

Herman Stone Company Office Building
　　The Herman Stone Company relocated from Dayton, Ohio to Mount Airy, North Carolina in the 1960's. They were the manufacturer of granite surface plates that played a vital role in precision production methods. They built their office building on the quarry property and later gave the building to North Carolina Granite. Mount Airy Granite Sawed Bed Ashlar was the main material used in the construction of their two story office building and plant. The base of the building was built with Cemesto with aluminum battens and a very light in color ashlar.

The former Herman Stone building located on the North Carolina Granite Quarry property, August 2011, Mount Airy, NC.

Herman Stone as it looks today from a distance.

This is a hand drawing found in the Mount Airy Broken Range Ashlar salesman's guide and entrance way with construction year at the main office building of the quarry.

Mr. And Mrs. Hemmings
Owners of Hemmings Grocery next to the quarry.

CHAPTER 2

Cape Fear and the Yadkin Valley Railroad

The original charter for this railroad was issued around 1829. The idea had developed in 1814 to connect the Yadkin Valley with Fayetteville and the Cape Fear River area. In 1879, once the last charter was issued then construction was completed without much interruption. Nearly sixty years before its completion, ground breaking occurred in Fayetteville. Apparently, financing of this project was difficult because the State did not provide resources for the work and locals were skeptical about donating their land for the project. They saw it as an experiment that would not work.

There was a time when the construction lay dormant for about 20 years. More than likely this was during and after the Civil War. Construction techniques at this time were crude and all work done by hand. This further hindered the speed of construction.

On February 25, 1879, reconstruction was seen as complete enough for the State government and a new grant was issued to merge the Mount Airy and Western Railroads, thus forming the Cape Fear and Yadkin Valley Railway Company (CF & YVR). With each general Assembly meeting after this, the state slowly released bits and pieces of ownership in the railroad to the company. On April 6, 1881, the company leadership dove into a contract with another company, Fayetteville and Florence Railroad, to complete the next segment to the South Carolina state line. This section was over an already graded road bed of the Cape Fear and Yadkin Valley to Shoe Heel which intersected with the Carolina Central Railway. At the same time construction began westward from the City of Greensboro to Robeson County.

By December 5th, 1884, construction was complete on the segment to Bennettsville, South Carolina; one hundred and fifty- four miles. This completion included train depots that were constructed by Thomas Woodroffe and sons, stock supplies, warehouses, and freight houses. Later connections were made to the Richmond and Danville Railroad.

At this point in time Greensboro became very important because it was the junction point of the Richmond and Danville Railroad with the CF & YVR. Twenty-two passenger trains went through Greensboro each day in 1885. Today it is also the center of trade with a major airport and several interstate highways.

The Blue Ridge Mountains of North Carolina were still out of reach. Construction was more difficult through the mountains requiring heavier blasting of the rock. On June 20th, 1888, The railway carried thousands of people to Mount Airy to celebrate the extension of the rails to this quaint foothills town. To many this was another world excursion. Before this time, travel to Mount Airy was slow at best due to the terrain.

With the rails complete to Mount Airy, the CF & YVR traversed through 19 counties. If you compare projects by the number of counties, then it compares to the Blue Ridge Parkway which today extends 469 miles through 19 counties from Waynesboro, Virginia to Cherokee, North Carolina.

The North State Improvement Company was credited with much of the work. Incorporated in 1883 by John D. Williams of Fayetteville (notice he was on the board of directors listed previously) and other men of high standings in North Carolina. The author notes that several of the men listed as directors were leaders in their communities and were an example of early American entrepreneurship. Their homes and business reflected their stature in the business world.

Above, this winter photo shows the rails from the CF and YV Railroad running into quarry. Courtesy of the Surry County Historical Society, Minick Collection.

Piedmont and Mount Airy Division (the Present Western Terminus of the Line)

Natural resources were treasured by the people of 1880s. Early records noted the farm lands that grew apples, cabbage, trees, vegetables, animals, tobacco, etc. This area was called "the Bright Tobacco Belt." This area was especially good for growing Bright Leaf Tobacco.

Reaching Mount Airy put visitors within five miles of the base of the Blue Ridge Mountains. Growth in Mount Airy for the previous five years had tripled in part due to the roads that were built to Winston-Salem, Greensboro and up into Virginia to Galax, Hillsville, and Wytheville.

At the completion of the railroad to the foothills, Mount Airy had four cotton mills, three wool mills, eleven tobacco factories, four tobacco-sales warehouses, three wagon factories, and at least four saw mills with machine and blacksmith shops. This was the beginning of the furniture industry that flooded America a few years later.

Laurel Bluff Cotton Mills boasted two thousand spindles and forty-five looms used in the manufacturing of warp yarn and plaid fabrics. It was located one mile from the center of town. Everything used in the construction of the facility was taken from on site including the brick because it was located on the river. Employees were paid 40 cents per day and they employed fifty- five operators.

Three creeks with eight water mills served Mount Airy. The creeks were the Ararat River, Lovell's Creek, and Stewart's creek (named after the JEB Stuart family). The Ararat River was described in the CY & YVR book as "Rock Ribbed and Ancient as the Sun!"

Early photo of completed rails and crew at the quarry. You can see men standing on granite at the top right behind the building. Courtesy of the Surry County Historical Society and the Broughton Collection.

Above, Cape Fear and Yadkin Valley Railroad. Courtesy of the Surry County Historical Society Minick Collection.

Then Mount Airy depot then and now. Courtesy of the Surry County Historical Society

Train with load of Mount Airy Granite. Courtesy of the Surry County Historical Society Minick Collection.

Flat Rock or Granite City?

Located one mile from the center of town was a natural wonder called "Flat Rock" by the locals. Today it is known as the North Carolina Granite Corporation, a near perfect supply of granite. Stonemasons were able to split slabs of rock with remarkable ease and little expense. They did this without blasting powder.

Because of the quarry, Mount Airy got the nick name "Granite City."

Mr. Thomas Woodroffe had purchased this "Flat Rock" by this time and had a very prosperous business delivering granite to all regions of North Carolina, Virginia, South Carolina, and any other section of the country that was supplied with the railroad. The largest piece of granite cut at this point was 114 feet long. Every piece of masonry used for the Fayetteville Bridge over the Cape Fear River was from the "Flat Rock."

It is important to note that "Flat Rock" was the end of the line for the railroad. This leg of the railroad, the leg to the quarry, built in 1888; happened three years after the line to downtown Mount Airy was completed. Because of the heaviness of the granite, it only made sense to bring the line into the quarry to ship granite. In this area of Mount Airy, the Dinky Railroad that ran to Dan Valley paralleled the lines of the CF & YVR. The Dinky was narrow gauge.

This is the section of the last terminus of rails located on Riverside Drive leading to the Mount Airy Granite facility.

Here is an excerpt from a book written in 1889.

CAPE FEAR AND YADKIN VALLEY RAILWAY SYSTEM
(From Mount Airy at the base of the Blue Ridge to Wilmington, N.C.)
It's Origins, Construction, Connections, and Extensions.
Printed in Philadelphia
By Allen, Lane, and Scott Printers
South Fifth Street
1889

Organization of the

CAPE FEAR AND YADKIN VALLEY RAILWAY COMPANY
1889

Julius A. Gray..............................President
J. W. Fry....................................Gen'l Supt
Roger P. Atkinson....................Chief Engineer
Jno. M. Rose..............................Secretary
R.W. Bidgood............................Auditor
Jas. R Williams..........................Treasurer
W.E. Kyle..................................G.F. and P.A.
Geo. M. Rose.............................Attorney

Directors:

K. M. Murchison, New York   Chas. P. Stokes, Richmond, VA.
Jno. M. Worth, Asheboro, N.C.   W. A. Moore, Mount Airy, N.C.
W. A. Lash, Walnut Cove, N.C.   J. Turner Morehead,
                                                        Leakesville, N.C.
Julius A. Gray, Greensboro, N.C.   D. W. C. Benbow, GSO, NC
G. W. Williams, Wilmington, N.C.   Robt. T. Gray, Durham, N.C.
Jno. D. Williams, Fayetteville, N.C. E. J. Lilly, Fayetteville, N.C.

General Offices   Greensboro, N.C.
Presidents Office
Fayetteville, N.C.

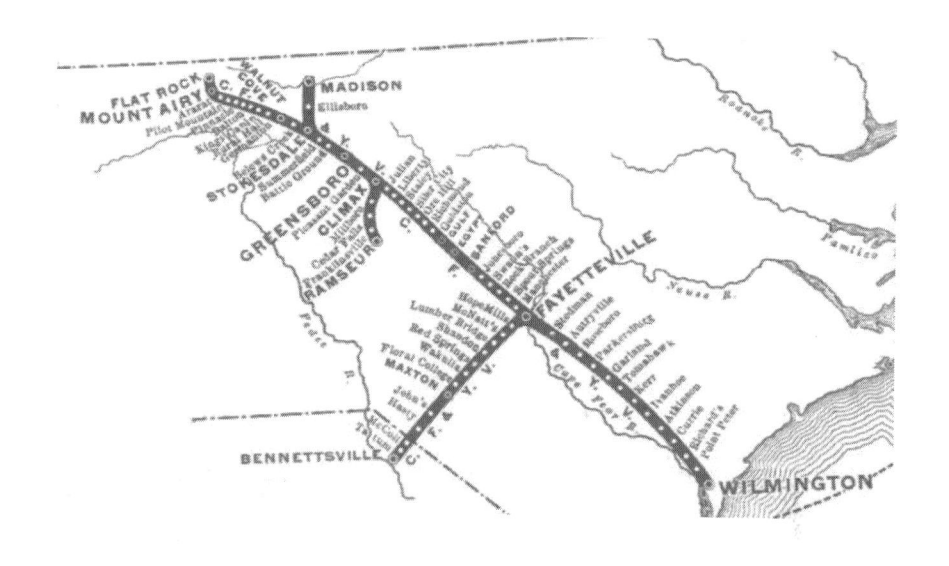

Drawing of the CF & YV Railway.

This is a vintage postcard of the rail line, sheds, and equipment loading granite in the shipping yard.

29

One of the many granite markers that can be found in Mount Airy.

Mount Airy has a wonderful park trail system including this one dedicated to H. B. Rowe. This park provides habitats for nature studies, exhibits for children about various plants or tree species native to the area. This was the first park in Mount Airy to be lit by solar lights.

CHAPTER 3

John Davis "Jack" Sargent

Jack Sargent joined the Mount Airy Granite Company in 1910 as an employee of Thomas Woodroffe, Jr. Quickly he climbed through the ranks and eventually bought the company forming the J. D. Sargent Granite Corporation (a separate company from the North Carolina Granite Corporation). This was in about 1918. During the 1920's Christopher Binder, born in Maine, was the General Manager; Robert Browne was the superintendent of finishing; William S. Martin was Secretary and Treasurer; and Raymond Sargent, son of Jack Sargent, was the Superintendent of the quarry.

Jack Sargent had an acute business sense. During his years of leadership, the company sales increased many times fold due to the marketing strategies he introduced. He personally visited clients, such as the Dodge Brothers in Detroit, Michigan. Sales folders were designed for the salesmen to share with their prospective customers.

To have had so many successful years as President of the North Carolina Granite Corporation one would expect a large mausoleum but instead he has a very nice twin crypt in the Oakdale Cemetery in Mount Airy, North Carolina. His crypt is of the art deco period with two large "vase like" statues at the end and of course it is made from solid Mount Airy Granite.

Jack was born in August 18, 1871 in Vermont and died May 24, 1945 in Mount Airy. He married Flora E. Kimbal (November 1, 1874 – October 28, 1962). His parents were Davis Sargent and Cordelia Dorche of Swanton Village in Franklin, Vermont. Davis Sargent was born in Canada.

The Jack Sargent home located on Main Street, Mount Airy, NC. Now a law office.

Above: Another view of the John Davis "Jack" Sargent and Flora Kimball Sargent Crypt located in the Oakdale Cemetery, Mount Airy, NC.

CHAPTER 4

Master Stonecutters

Stone Masonry has been around since the beginning of time therefore making it one of the oldest careers known to man. It has been used to create sculpture, buildings, bridges, and other structures. Many of the world's long lasting monuments and memorials were created by stone masons. For example the Taj Mahal, the Roman Coliseum, Egyptian Pyramids, and Stonehenge are great examples of things crafted from stone.

Medieval stone masons were in high demand for their skills. Being a member of the guild (which required years of apprenticing) gave rise to three classes of stone masons: apprentices, journeymen, and the master masons. In ancient times it took seven years to apprentice. With the development of technology and better tools that was cut to four years. Depending on the skills of the person today it may be shorter but involves learning high tech drafting and computer equipment.

The definition of a stone mason or stonecutter is someone that shapes rough pieces of stone into accurate geometrical shapes, some simple, some not so simple, then arranging them in order, usually, with mortar, to form structures. Throughout this book you will see great examples of structures created with Mount Airy Granite.

Some terms to be familiar with include quarrymen, sawyers, banker masons, carvers, fixer masons, and memorial masons. There are also different levels to becoming a licensed mason, too. Today as in the past, the stonecutter goes through extensive training and apprenticeship to become licensed and accepted in their field.

The quarrymen's job is to split the rock and extract it from the ground.

A sawyer then cuts these blocks into cubes with diamond tip saws.

A Banker Mason works in the shop cutting and carving the stone into intricate moulding, doorways, and basic building blocks.

The carver steps over the line into the field of art and carves the stone into an artistic item like a statue, or details for a building like gargoyles, animals, and foliage (which is very popular).

Fixer masons are specialists in putting the stones, mouldings, etc. onto the buildings using special mortars. Sometimes metal fixtures are used. This is a highly skilled job because it requires a high degree of knowledge of precise tolerance.

Last, but not least, are the memorial masons that carve tombstones. To the general public they are the most well known.

Like artists today sign their work, medieval stonemasons would carve a personal symbol on their work to differentiate their work.

Stonemasons use all types of stones. For example they might use igneous, metamorphic and sedimentary; while some also use artificial stone as well. Granite is igneous rock and is the toughest thus making it great for structural support. That would be why it is used as cornerstones for many buildings. If you walk up and down Main Street Mount Airy you can look at the old store fronts and see the granite cornerstones even if the rest of the building is brick.

Two types of stone masonry exist; rubble masonry and ashlar masonry. Rubble masonry is a rough stone that is joined to another stone with mortar, and then finished with another product on the outside. Ashlar masonry has a finished look about it and is used in retaining walls, homes, and buildings. No other product is needed to cover it up. Typically they are contrasted with other material. Some homes will have an ashlar granite foundation and brick going up the rest of the way. The contrast of different materials is the beauty of this type of construction.

Mortar is the substance that binds all of these rocky materials together. When cured it hardens solid and holds everything in place. In modern times it usually includes sand, a binder such as cement, and water. The combination of the sand type and the binder give it unique colors. Ancient mortar was made with clay and water.

Scalpellini (stonecutters) migrated from northern Italy to Mount Airy, North Carolina, Barre, Vermont, and other communities that had quarries at the turn of the century. They were assertive and effective laborers. In the beginning their work mimicked what they knew from Europe but eventually they created unique architecture.

The 20th Century brought radical change to the industry with the creation of steam equipment and compressed air tools. Formerly they used draft animals and muscle power. With the steam engine came first the railroad and then the heavy lifting equipment. Forklifts and cranes revolutionized the moving aspect of the job. Electric saws cut the time down drastically from hand chiseling.

Stonecutters from many parts of Europe brought this tradition of autonomy to the United States and were willing to assert their rights in American workplaces. These Italians were at the forefront of the

American labor movement's struggle for fairer and safer working conditions, like shorter hours and better working environments. According to Chicago sculptor Walter Arnold, the Journeymen's Stonecutters Association of North America (now merged with the Laborers), is among the oldest continuously operating international union in the country, founded in 1853.

Immigrant stonecutters exhibited hope as Jeremiah had hope that he would be molded by God's own hand as the potter molded the clay, the stonecutters cut the granite. Not everyone is cut out to be a stonecutter. It is a calling and a specialty that takes years to master.

Vincenzo "Big Jim" Alfano (1884 - 1947) came to America in 1903 and was a master stone cutter with the North Carolina Granite Corporation. Courtesy of the Mount Airy Museum of Regional History.

Stone carvings created by "Big Jim" Alfano that stood in his front yard along West Pine Street. Courtesy of the Surry County Historical Society, Minick Collection.

The former Alfano home that was located on West Pine Street in Mount Airy. Note the stone carved granite planter next to the tree. Courtesy of the Surry County Historical Society from the Minick Collection.

The former Alfano home that was located on West Pine Street in Mount Airy. Note the stone carved granite planter next to the tree. Courtesy of the Surry County Historical Society from the Minick Collection.

Vincenzo "Big Jim" Alfano and son, Ugo Alfano, standing next to one of his granite creations, a hanging basket holder. Ugo was a textile consultant/salesman for Renfro Manufacturing in Mount Airy, NC. He and his wife had two children and six grandchildren. Courtesy of the Mount Airy Museum of Regional History.

Ugo Alfano and his mother, Martha Alfano, standing next to one of Big Jim's granite creations, a very large planter then and now. Courtesy of the Mount Airy Museum of Regional History.

Martha Avello Alfano (1884-1939), wife of Vincenzo "Big Jim" Alfano.
Courtesy of the Mount Airy Museum of Regional History

The Alfano Family granite tombstone located in Oakdale Cemetery, carved by Edward Alfano.

Another view of the Alfano family granite tombstone with one of Big Jim's planters.

Master Carvers standing next to copolla's carved for New York Municiple Building. Courtesy of the Surry County Historical Society Minick Collection

Stonecutters of Mount Airy

Footstone of Pietro D'Amico in Oakdale Cemetery.
Pietro D'Amico was born on April 29, 1887 in Alfedana L'Aquila, Italy and was a retired paving cutter from the North Carolina Granite Corporation. His funeral services were held at the Holy Angels Catholic Church by Father Becker.

This is the headstone for the D'Amico family and it is located in Oakdale Cemetery.

Marcelino San Emeterio came from Spain and was a stonecutter. His footstone (not of granite) says, Q.E.P.D. which stands for *"que en paz descanse"* which means *"rest in peace."*

Stone Cutters Union, the banner reads "Mount Airy Branch of Granite Cutters."Courtesy of the Surry County Historical Society, Minick Collection.

More on the History of Stone Cutters

Immigrants to Mount Airy came from primarily four countries Italy, Scotland, England, and Germany. Most were trained in their home country or in other Granite Quarries before arriving in Surry County.

It took the Scotchman who knew how to get the stone out of the ground using black powder. They knew how to get it out in any size. They were not as skilled in the artisitic side of carving like Michelangelo.

So from Italy came the fine carvers line the Valentines, D'Amicos, Da Palmos, Alfanos, and Biancos. In the DaPalma family were born eight boys. Six of those eight became stone cutters with the Mount Airy Granite. Vincenzo Alfano rests in the Oak Dale Cemetery underneath a stone carved by his son, Edward Alfano, by far one of the classiest pieces of art in Mount Airy Proper.

Quote from a quarry official, "Labor is native efficient and satisfied. It is not unusual to find grandfathers, fathers, and sons, working side by side."

In the 1920's only twenty-seven Scotts remained in the area.

In the 1930's, the Scottish immigrant population was declining in Mount Airy. Only nine can be found on the census. This was due in part to the opening of other quarries in the U.S. and also due to the Union organizations. Some were for it and others were opposed. Of course management opposed the union but it was organized anyway. Later it was disorganized and reorganized again. Because of the bitter conflict many found it better to move on. The economy was rocky in the 1920's thus leading them to go where the work could be found.

This group of stone cutters was fairly mobile and records show that they travelled the rails where ever the work took them. Some of them were in Danville, Virginia at one point. They were hired to build a dam for one of the cotton mills and later built at least three granite homes before moving on. Before coming to Mount Airy, many of these workers had already been to Massachusetts, Ohio, Georgia, Vermont, and Virginia. When they left, they went back to some of these quarries and to others in Kentucky, Georgia, and Ohio.

In 1905, the Stone Cutters Union participated in a parade in downtown Mount Airy. Courtesy of the Surry County Historical Society, Minick Collection.

James David Thompson

The Thompson Inn was built by James David Thompson. He was born on May 22, 1868 in Scotland. In 1880, At the age of 22 he came to Massachusetts. Sometime around 1890 he married Margaret "Maggie" Morrice who was born in 1874 in Aberdeen Scotland. To this union was born a daughter, Christobel "Christie" Thompson in 1891. Christie was born in Massachusetts. Likely they met in Massachusetts. A year later their daughter Maggie was born in Vermont. Sometime around 1900 or 1901 they migrated to Mount Airy.

James was a stone cutter. While he worked, Maggie ran the Thompson Boarding House. Very soon after construction they boarded Scottish immigrant quarry workers. By 1907 they built an even bigger boarding home. Today the second construction is still located on Pine Street. This home was large and in 1910 the census shows it holding twenty-one total; four of them are the Thompson family. For the remainder of their lives this was their home. They are buried in Oakdale Cemetery. Maggie died in 1959 and James in 1948. Christie never married. She died in 1974. Maggie, their daughter, married George Mitchell in 1918. He was a paving cutter at the quarry. They remained in the Thompson home until their death.

As with the McKellars and others, the Thompson Family was charter members of the Flat Rock Presbyterian Church. It is within walking distance.

The Thompson House

CHAPTER 5

Harry Barton (1876-1937)

A native of Philadelphia, Pennsylvania, Harry Barton moved to Greensboro, North Carolina in 1912 to practice his trade of architecture. He moved with his wife, Rachel Phillips Barton, because he felt that Greensboro was a "city with a future and convenient to one of the most prosperous regions in the entire Piedmont section." Barton joined an established firm of Frank A. Weston, who had practiced architecture in Denver, Colorado, a few years earlier.

Harry attended public school in Philadelphia. Then he attended Williamson School and Temple College, and George Washington University where he received his formal architectural education. After his graduation he took special coursework in architectural design at the Beaux Art Institute of Design which is located in New York City.

Being religious and civic minded he joined the First Presbyterian Church and eventually became an elder in the church. This was only after 5 years in Greensboro. Widely respected in the community, Barton became a Mason, a president of the Kiawanis club, mayor of Hamilton Lakes suburb, and a member of several other civic groups.

Soon he established his own practice with a large client base among the city's leaders. Once established a few years, he secured the contract to build the very large, neoclassical Guilford Courthouse (1918-1920). Although his business centered in Greensboro, it also covered other North Carolina towns, schools, and communities. During the roaring 20's, Harry Barton was the leading architect in Greensboro.

The grave of Architect Harry Barton in Forest Lawn Cemetery, Greensboro, North Carolina. Notice that although he built many items with Mount Airy Granite, his tombstone and footstone are carved from marble.

Guilford County Courthouse designed by Harry Barton.

Barton was one of the first licensed Architects in North Carolina. Issued in 1915, his license number was #44 in the registration book for the North Carolina Board of Architecture. He was one of the few in the early group of licensed architects in the state based on the fact that they had been in a professional practice prior to the licensing act of 1915. He was a member of the American Institute of Architects, a member of the North Carolina Chapter of American Institute of Architects, and president in 1932-1933, leading it through the worst years of the Great Depression, and he was also the secretary of the State Board of Examiners in Architecture.

Barton incorporated Mount Airy Granite in many of his buildings. Some in the following list are totally constructed with granite. Most have some granite in the design.

Known Buildings by Harry Barton:
Almanace County Courthouse (Graham, NC); Alleghany County Courthouse (1933, Sparta, NC); Charles W. McCrary House (1929, Asheboro, Randolph County, NC); Church of the Covenant, a Presbyterian Church (1914, Greensboro, NC); Cone Export and Commission Building (1924, Greensboro, NC); Cumberland County Courthouse (1924); Ferndale Junior High School (1931, High Point, NC); First Methodist Church (1924, Asheboro, NC); First Baptist Church (1927, Siler City, NC); First Presbyterian Church (1927-1928, High Point); Galen Stone Hall (1927, Palmer Institute, Sedalia, NC); Granite Lodge No. 322 (1931, Mount Airy, NC); Greensboro City Hall (1924, Greensboro, NC); Greensboro Daily News Building (1924, Greensboro, NC); Guilford County Courthouse (1920's, Greensboro); Guilford County Home for the Aged and Infirmed (Ca. 1922, Greensboro, NC); Harry Barton House (1927, 104 Kemp Road, Greensboro, NC); High Point Central High School (1927, High Point, NC); J.M. Galloway House (1919, Greensboro, NC); John W. King House (1914, Greensboro, NC); Johnston County Courthouse (1921, Johnston, NC); Meyer's Department Store (1924, Greensboro, NC); Morrison- Neese Furniture Building (Ca. 1924, Greensboro, NC); Piedmont Building (1927, Greensboro, NC); Pilot Life Insurance Co. Complex (1927-1928, Greensboro, NC); Reidsville Municipal Building (1926, Reidsville, NC); S.H. Tomlinson House (1924, High Point, NC); Sigmund Sternberger House (1925, Greensboro, NC); Sedgefield Country Club (1927, Greensboro, NC); Surry County Courthouse (1916, Dobson); W.W. Graves House (1922, Wilson, NC); World War Memorial Stadium (1926, Greensboro, NC); YMCA Building (1915, Greensboro, NC); YWCA Building (1920s, Greensboro, NC).

In 1921, Harry Barton received a commission for the expansion on the campus of the University of North Carolina at Greensboro. During this time, the state invested in and educational building campaign. Julius Foust, UNCG college president, commissioned Barton to design seventeen of the thirty buildings on campus. These buildings were constructed of red brick by the J. A. Jones Construction Company of Charlotte, North Carolina. He used Mount Airy Granite to accentuate and highlight the windows, steps, doorways, and sidewalks.

UNCG Buildings:
Chancellor's House (1923)
Aycock Auditorium (1927)
Bailey Dormitory (1922)
Brown Music Building (1924)
Coit Dormitory (1923)
Cotton Dormitory (1922)
Foust Dormitory (1928)
Gray Dormitory (1921)
New Curry Education Bldg. (1926)
South Dining Hall (1924)
Stone Economics Building (1928)
West Dining Hall (1921)
Guilford Dormitory (1928)
Hinshaw Dormitory (1922)
Jamison Dormitory (1923)
Rosenthal Gym (1925)
Shaw Dormitory (1920)

The Julius I. Foust Building at UNCG is one of the original buildings of the university. It was comleted in 1892 and has been on the list of National Register of Historic Places since 1980. Dr. Foust was the 2nd President of the school, then named The North Carolina Normal and Industrial College.

Another view of the granite arches built on the Foust Building at UNCG.

CHAPTER 6

Tesh Lumber Company and Joseph A. Tesh

Joseph Alexander Tesh (July 24, 1865 – June 10, 1944) was born to Romulus Bradbury Tesh, a Civil War Veteran, in Davie County, North Carolina. His mother was Abergale Greene Tesh. She was a descendant of Nathaniel Greene, a Revolutionary War Patriot. J.A. was a descendent of the first Tesch that came to America and settled in what is now Welcome, North Carolina, Heinrich Tesch. Heinrich was one of the founding fathers of the Friedburg Moravian Church.

Joseph's early career was as a carpenter for the granite quarry in Mount Airy. Next he took up contracting carpenter jobs, moving around the area. Legend has it that he built every railroad station from Wilmington, NC to Key West, FL. Knowing the history of the Thomas Woodroffe and Sons lumber company, I would speculate that he partnered with Thomas when Thomas got the contract from the Cape Fear and Yadkin Valley Railroad to build all of the train depots from Mount Airy to Wilmington. While working on the coast, Joseph carried his lumber by Schooner down the coastal waterways. If he worked for Thomas he used the rails from Mount Airy to get the lumber to the coast.

Joseph built the granite railroad station in Mount Airy. Today it is vacant but still very quaint and symbolizes Mount Airy and prosperity.

While in Wilmington, Joseph met his beloved, Mary Catherine Lewis, the daughter of a Civil War Veteran, Marshall Owen Lewis. They were betrothed on August 29, 1894, moved to Mount Airy and spent the rest of their lives there raising a family and conducting business.

Once returning to Mount Airy, Joseph went to work for the quarry at $9.00 per week. In 1900 he started the Tesh Lumber Company. In conjunction with contractors he provided lumber for or was instrumental in the construction of several buildings in Mount Airy. They include, but at not limited to, the Allen House in Fancy Gap, Virginia, Trinity Episcopal Church on Main Street, the Maxwell Boarding House on North Main Street, the Raymond Tesh home that was formerly located beside the Holy Angels Catholic Church, and all of the depots from Mount Airy to Wilmington, and very possibly other little buildings along the way.

J.A. Tesh was also one of the founders of the Workman's Federal Savings and Loan.

He lived a very productive long life.

Joseph A. Tesh in his Masonic Uniform.
Courtesy of Craig and Jane Culler Tesh

Joseph A. and Mary Catherine Tesh photo.
Courtesy of Craig and Jane Culler Tesh

The Walkertown Depot that was built with lumber from Tesh Lumber Company.

To the left of the Davidson Arch in this vintage postcard of the Guilford Courthouse Battleground/Military Park was the old depot that was probably built by J. A. Tesh Lumber Company. The little building to the right was the first museum which he may have also constructed. The CF & YV railway ran between the two arches and is now Old Battleground Road.

CHAPTER 7

Granite Buildings in Mount Airy

This is the granite sign in front of the Flat Rock Ruritan building and the Flat Rock Ruritan building below.

The Rotary Club is part of a national organization. They have a common them, they take action in the community through volunteering. The club provides opportunities for interaction between civic leaders and business leaders, mentoring young people, and by providing support for needed projects in the community and throughout the world. It is open to everyone regardless of race or sex.

Community Scout Building

Built in 1950, the Scout House was built for the local chapter of Boy Scouts. Stone was donated by the North Carolina Granite Corporation. Ms. Peral Campbell razed the majority of the funding to buy the lumber and have the stone layed. Stonecutters on the project were Bob Loftis, Dennis Parries, A.P. Phillips, A. Lee Hiatt, Reynold McCoy, and Lacy McMillian. Mr. Otto Reeves layed the ashlar stone.

Former Moorefield Eye, Ear, Nose, and Throat Hospital

Dr. Laurimer Jennings (L.J.) Moorefield, Sr. was an ear, eye, nose, and throat specialist that moved to Mount Airy about 1916 as the corporate physician for the North Carolina Granite Corporation. In 1923, he erected a private hospital next to the Martin Memorial Hospital.

Although Dr. Moorefield specialized in eye, ear, nose, and throat problems, he delivered 5,000 babies in his lifetime.

He was born on a farm in Walnut Cove, North Carolina on January 6, 1888 to James William and Mary Willis Moorefield.

Dr. Moorefield was known for taking his horse and buggy or his Model T Ford for house calls. If they were not available he would walk. In his later years he maintained his office in his home. He did his premedical work at Guilford College and played baseball while there. He received his medical degree in 1913 from North Carolina Medical College in Charlotte, which later merged with the University of Virginia. Some of his post graduate work he did in New York and Chicago. Dr. Moorefield continued practice until his death in 1969.

The Moorefield Eye, Ear, Nose, and Throat Hospital erected in 1923.

Dr. Moorefield's tombstone in Oakdale Cemetery.

Dr. Ashby's tombstone in Oakdale Cemetery.

    Opening in 1918, the Martin Memorial Hospital School of Nursing had five students in the first class. They graduated in 1921. Overall from the opening until it closed on May 1, 1953, they graduated over 250 nursing students.
    The former Martin Memorial Hospital closed on May 1, 1953 due to a fire. All of the patients were evacuated to the nearby Reeves Community Center. For four years, patients had to travel nearly 40 miles

if they needed a hospital, either to Elkin or to Winston - Salem.

The new hospital opened on April 1, 1957 with 98 beds. In 1969, it expanded with a 24 hour emergency room.

One of the most well known teaching doctors was Dr. Roy C. Mitchell.

The Former Martin Memorial Hospital

Mrs. B. A. Irvin built this hospital for her son who was a physician. They owned and operated it for a very short time and then Dr. Moir S. Martin purchased the property from her in 1915 and renamed it for his father, Dr. R. S. Martin who was from Stuart, Virginia. Sometime in the 1920's, Dr. Martin took on a business partner, Dr. Edward C. Ashby, who was a surgeon, also.

This is a vintage postcard view of the Martin Memorial Hospital, front view, dating back to the 1920's. Courtesy of the Surry County Historical Society

This is a vintage linen postcard, rearview of the Martin Memorial Hospital dating somewhere in the 1920's or 1930's. Courtesy of the Surry County Historical Society from the Minick Collection

Martin Memorial Hospital burned on May 1, 1953. The granite building was 40 years old at this point. The fireman concluded that it was electrical in nature and started near the chimney at the Obstetrics section of the hospital. Firemen had the fire under control until the blaze reached a supply of ether. The explosion pretty much destroyed the building. Miraculously, no one was injured and all 61 patients were transferred to Reeves Community Center. Dr. Martin was out of town but left immediately and came back to Mount Airy. His report to the Winston-Salem Journal on May 3, 1953 said that the evacuation went as planned and that the staff operated in a very professional manner without causing panic.

    Several of the patients were transferred to Winston-Salem hospitals (seven to the City Memorial Hospital and four to Baptist Hospital) during the early morning hours of May 2. The community pulled together during this disaster and brought food and water to the patients, staff, and safety officials. Some even took patients to their homes.

    Dr. Martin quickly began to push forward the plans of the new hospital. Within two days he had secured the help of the state Medical Care Commission with 33 percent of the funding provided. The Medical Care Commission approved a 100 bed hospital, although Dr. Martin said that a larger was needed. Also, the County Board of Commissioners met in Dobson for a bond referendum hearing, led by a local attorney, Fred Folger, board of trustee member for the hospital. The estimated total funds needed for the new hospital were 1.8 million dollars.

Another uncertainty was the nurse's school that was ran by Mrs. Bertha Ashby, superintendent of nurses. Graduation was scheduled for May 19th. She continued the graduation plans for the seniors. The 25 freshman and juniors had to be transferred to another program at another school. Most of the student nurses were given the weekend off after the fire to go home and rest and visit with their families. They had pulled several 24 hour shifts at the Community Center taking care of patients.

There were 15 graduate nurses and 34 student nurses on duty at the time of the fire.

The new hospital was dedicated on March 31, 1957. Governor Luther H. Hodges dedicated the new hospital and nurse's home, costing $1,850,000. Governor Hodges credited Dr. Martin with "invaluable leadership" in the construction of the new hospital "pouring his life, his talents, and his dreams into serving health needs among Surry County residents."

Dr. Moir Martin, son of Dr. Richard Saunders Martin and Emma Moir Martin, was born in Stokes County, North Carolina on January 20, 1883. He died on January 4, 1960 while his wife was having surgery in the very hospital that he founded. She was unable to attend his funeral. They were married in 1907.

Dr. Martin received his early education at the Danville Military Institute, Danville, Virginia. He attended Hampden- Sydney College in Virginia and received his medical degree from the Medical College of Virginia in 1905.

He had memberships in many organizations including Phi Chi medical fraternity, Kappa Sigma, the Masons, the Surry County Medical Society, the Medical Society of North Carolina, the Virginia Medical Association, the Southeastern Surgical Congress, and he was the past president and founder of the Mount Airy Kiwanis Club.

He was surgeon for the Southeastern Railway and a former member of the Surry County Highway Commission.

He always wore a red rose in his lapel.

This is a current view of the former Martin Memorial Hospital. It has been recycled and converted into apartments.

In this photo above, Kiwanis Picnic at White Sulphur Springs Motel. Many of the Mount Airy physicians and dentists were founding members of the Kiwanis Club. Photo courtesy of the Surry County Historical Society from the Minick Collection

Front row, left to right: G.C. Lovill, E.C. Bivens, E. C., George K. Snow,

Earl Wray, C. Wray, Roy Edwards, Jessee Simmons, John D. Thompson (Possible Stonecutter), H. H. Llewellyn, Dr. Hege, T.G. Fawcett, Lib Fawcett.

Sceond row: D.H. cook, Dr. Green, C.W. Andrew, W. S. Wolfe, Lucien Wrenn, Stephen M. Hale, Wiley Dobbins, J. H. Folger, 9(?), 10(?), 11(?), Blair Hines, Blair, Miss Kelly, C. H. Haynes, D.F. Hoffman, Ed Linville, W. J. Byerly.

Third row: R.V. Dyerly, J.S. Bray, Fred Folger, C. Binder, W. E. Lindsey, Fred Blevins, Ross Ashby, Claude Absher, Dr. Mitchell, Hugh Holcomb, Hendren, W. S. Ashby, (?) Judson, Wayne Christian, Vance Haynes, G. K. Hale, Dr. Moir Martin (founder of the Mount Airy Kiwanis Club), Le Roy (Raleigh) Marlin, (AST. C.)
Doughlery, L. B. Pendergraph, Will Johnson, 21(?), Claude Flippin, Bob Brown, J. B. Sparger, A.B. Webb, George Hutchins, W. G. Sydnor.

Reeves Community Center

Reeves Community Center, opened in 1953, serves the community as the local YMCA. It is a public, nonprofit corporation. The front of the building is Mount Airy Granite. It is located on the corner of Pine Street and Renfro Street in Mount Airy. They offer a wide variety of athletic and health related activities.

On May 1, 1953, the Martin Memorial Hospital burned and all of the 61 patients were transferred here. For several days, Reeves was set up as a temporary hospital. Four babies were born here during that event;

one was transferred to Dr. Mitchell's office.

The four infants were brought into life at Reeves Community Center. The first child was born to Mr. and Mrs. Billy Marion (transferred to Dr. Mitchell's office), Miss Tiny Susan Rae Taylor, daughter of Mr. and Mrs. Ray Taylor of Mount Airy. The second child was born to Mrs. William Scott of Mount Airy. Mrs. Scott told the reporter with the Winston-Salem Journal that the fire gave her baby "a hot start in life." The fourth child born was a baby girl to Mrs. Calvin McHone.

John Reeves of New York City for whom Reeves Community Center is named after.
Surry County Historical Society from the Minick Collection

Former Bank of Mount Airy that was organized in 1905 by W. J. Byeryly. This building was erected in 1923.

Former First National Bank built in 1893

This is the foundation of the Emporium Building in Mount Airy.

Store front located on Main Street, Mount Airy.

Now Holcomb Hardware, this was once Hale Drygoods.

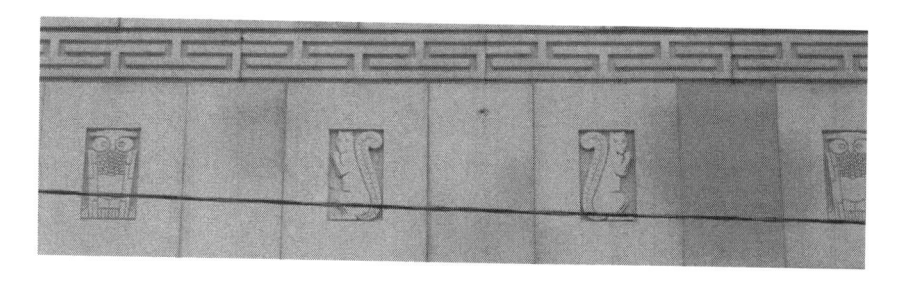

Detailed carvings of owls and squirrels located on the former Federal Savings and Loan building located at 218 N. Main Street, Mt. Airy.

Close up of the Mount Airy Post Office

The Mount Airy post office was designed by Geroge R. Berryman and constructed in 1932 on the southeast corner of South Main and Pine Street. Vincenzo "Big Jim" Alfano, an Italian stonecutter, executed the carvings in the Art Deco style of the 1930s. It has stylized floral motifs and bands of low relief geometrical designs ornament the smooth.

Intricate moulding carved over the front door of the post office in the photo above.

The photo below shows the Grecian fret, or key pattern. These are produced by dividing the height into any number of equal parts, and the horizontal line into the same divisions; then draw the lines through, intersecting each other, forming small squares, and then trace the pattern, then bands and sinkings being of equal width.

Vintage linen postcard of the Mount Airy Post Office.

Hand carved grape leaves found on a mausoleum.

The old spring/well house located at the quarry across from the main office. Notice the horse trough underneath the faucet.

James Clyde Hicks (1910-1978) and Hubert Comer shaking hands in front of the trough in the photo above.

Ode to Granite

Cut into piles of blocks
You are not just any rock,
You took my imagination
And gave me writers hope.

I seized the creative idea
Slowly mulling it over until light.
Out of the granite like a sphinx
As if carved by the stonecutters extinct.

You grasped my imagination
And threw me into a world of unknown stone.
Slowly sculpting my design
Into a literary mine.

I think granite is grand
When others think it is bland.
Every piece was carved by hand
Sweetly by the stone man.

My eyes search for the next piece of art
And they are trained in your fine details.
Not hidden by God
But carved for the world to see.

When our paths again collide
And I see your gleaming pride,
My mind will fly
As ideas again take flight.

Karen J. Hall

CHAPTER 8

Mausoleums of the Famous and Not So Famous

The Egyptian Pyramids, the Taj Mahal, and the Catacombs are all well known mausoleums designed centuries ago. While all are built to protect the remains of famous people and show their position in power, they, also in fact, state that the person wants to be memorialized.

What is a mausoleum?

The mausoleum gets its name from King Mausolus, whom was encrypted in grand style by his queen in the 19th century. As old church cemeteries were getting filled this was an alternative solution for saving space. Large community mausoleums share the costs and make the burial process more affordable for the average person. For example see the photo of the community mausoleum below.

As we know it today, mausoleums are buildings built by contractors like the North Carolina Granite Corporation that house the remains of individuals. The building is sturdy and made from cement or stone such as granite, and weather proof. They come in various sizes. Some hold two people others hold a full community. Typically they are located within a cemetery and are strategically placed for a grand view. Located above ground they provide a resting place for those that do not want to be buried. Land is saved because several burials can go up versus taking up several plots in a cemetery.

What is the difference between a cemetery and a graveyard?

If graves are in the church yard it is a graveyard. If graves are elsewhere it is a cemetery.

Vestibule Design

The Estate Vestibule Design appears to be the most popular design in Virginia and North Carolina. The pre-constructed or prefabricated vestibule mausoleum provides for the interment of one to six family members.

This mausoleum is designed like a small church. Usually it has two columns on the outside with a "church" door leading into the mausoleum. The door, usually made of metal, sometimes has a window to look into the vestibule. Some have no windows such as the Fries

Mausoleum in the Winston-Salem City Cemetery.

A vestibule allows private, personal meditation and a means of continued memorialization by family and loved ones. In other words, visitors may enter the vestibule and place flowers upon the crypts or leave them in the middle for a memorial. Constructed from beautiful, solid granite, each design is individually assembled into a single structure and delivered in one complete unit, ready for placement on the cemetery property. On site assembly is not required.

The Estate Vestibule Design can be personalized with different roof designs, carvings on the outer walls, and stained glass windows. Urns and vases can be added for a personal touch.

Located in the Oakwood Cemetery in High Point, NC, the D. Williams mausoleum is a great example of an estate design that is decorated with statues, carvings, and a granite retaining wall.

A Lasting Remembrance

From ancient days to present, the individual or family mausoleum has been regarded among the finest forms of burial. The tranquility of personal mausoleums is often a deciding factor for many families. The rich granite color and personalized inscriptions symbolize family pride. The founding fathers of the NCGC have utilized the granite material to the fullest.

Former Owners of North Carolina Granite Corporation
The "Big Four"

1. John D. "Jack" Sargent

Jack Sargent joined the Mount Airy Granite Company in 1910 as an employee of Thomas Woodroffe, Jr. Quickly he climbed through the ranks and eventually bought the company forming the J. D. Sargent Granite Corporation. This was in about 1918.

To have had so many successful years as President of the North Carolina Granite Corporation one would expect a large mausoleum but instead he has a very nice twin crypt in the Oakdale Cemetery in Mount Airy, North Carolina. His crypt is of the art deco period with two large "vase like" statues at the end. Of course it is made from solid Mount Airy Granite.

2. William Francis Shaffner and Son

Born September 20, 1869 in Winston-Salem, Forsyth County, North Carolina, William F. Shaffner was the son of a successful Civil War physician, Dr. Joseph Shaffner and Carrie Fries Shaffner. He was the nephew of Col. Francis Fries and became his protégé in the banking business. Mr. Shaffner was president of what we know today as Wachovia Bank and Trust.

During the 1920's he owned one quarter interest in the North Carolina Granite Corporation. It was during this time period that his mausoleum was designed. The Shaffner mausoleum still sustains a wonderful lasting beauty with a stained glass window of Lilies of the Valley.

William "Bill" F. Shaffner, Jr., a Rotarian, became instrumental in the preservation of Old Salem. Bill, as he was called, was appointed by the city alderman to do a study of Salem on October 21, 1947. He felt that this committee could come to a conclusion of preserving the community. The new Citizens Committee for Preservation of Historic Salem had much going for it and left us a wonderful legacy. If you walk around the Salem community and campus of Salem College, you will see many details that were constructed of Mount Airy Granite. No doubt, part of this was due to the family connection with the company.

The Bill Shaffner Mausoleum is located in the Salem City Cemetery.

3. **Col. Francis "Frank" Fries**

During the 1920's Col. Francis Fries obtained one quarter ownership in the North Carolina Granite Corporation. The Fries family Vault/Mausoleum is made of North Carolina Granite. Several of the Fries family members (about eight) are buried in the mausoleum in Salem Cemetery. The Fries Family Mausoleum is unique in that it is placed into the side of a hill with only the front being made from granite. The door has no window and is solid metal. As can be seen in the photo, the entranceway is arched like a rainbow.

Colonel Francis Fries was born on February 1, 1855 and died on June 5, 1931. Col. Fries was not actually a colonel but given the title by the North Carolina Governor as a distinction of honor for all of his community service during his life. Once receiving this title he used it to distinguish himself from his father, Francis L. Fries, another successful business man from Winston-Salem, North Carolina. His mother was Lezetta Vogler of the well known Moravian Vogler silversmith family.

Mr. Fries attended the Salem Boys School and later graduated from Davidson College in 1874. His career resembled that of his father, who founded the first successful textile mill in Salem, North Carolina. The Fries Manufacturing Company was built in 1839 by his father and became the F and H Fries Manufacturing Company in 1846, and was operated until 1928. It produced the famous "Salem Jeans." Fries, like his brothers, became a partner in the firm at age twenty-one; he was superintendent until 1887. In 1881 he built Arista Mills, the first mill in North Carolina to have electric lights. Shortly afterward, he started the Indera Mills. The first electric plant in North Carolina still stands in the forks of the road near Brookstown Avenue in Winston-Salem.

Col. Fries first married Anna DeSchwinitz. They had one child that did not make it to adulthood. When Anna died he then married Letitia Walker Patterson. They had several children.

Before becoming the President of Wachovia Bank and Trust Co., Col. Fries was a prominent Railroad man and Textile entrepreneur. It was the largest bank in the south and the largest bank between New Orleans and Baltimore.

In 1887, R. J. Reynolds and others urged Fries to assume the task of building a 122-mile railroad to cross the mountains to connect Winston and Salem, North Carolina to Roanoke, Virginia. This spur of railroad was completed in 1891 at a cost of $2 million. The Roanoke and

Southern Railway, which Fries served at times as president and general manager, became part of the Norfolk and Western rail system in 1892.

Plans to build another line from Winston and Salem to Wadesboro, North Carolina, in order to connect with the Atlantic Coastline Railroad were postponed because of the depression of the 1890s. Later, Fries helped his brother, Henry Elias Fries, then president of the Winston-Salem Southbound Railroad, complete the line to Wadesboro, North Carolina. The purpose of these rail lines was to prevent Winston and Salem from being commercially isolated. This allowed for a growth boom of the twenties.

Henry E. Fries formed the Fries Manufacturing and Power Company with his uncle and brothers, John W. and Francis H. Fries. They bought rights to the electric street cars and built the third electric street car system in America. Richmond, Virginia and Montgomery, Alabama were the first two. Next they bought a charter for a hydroelectric plant which they placed on the Yadkin River at a place called Douthit's Shoals. This land was owned by Uncle Henry Fries. On April 18, 1898, Little Marguerite Fries, daughter of Henry E. and Rosa Fries, flipped the switch that ran power 14 miles to Salem. The first cotton mill in America to have electric lights was the Arista Mills owned by Francis L. Fries. Fries Manufacturing and Power existed until 1913 when James B. Duke, president of Southern Power Company, purchased the stock. He then formed the Southern Public Utilities Company.

A very important aspect of Henry E. Fries' life happened in 1893 when he went into banking as president of the first trust company in North Carolina, the Wachovia Loan and Trust Company that had been organized in 1891 by his uncle Henry, his brother John, and others. In 1911, this company joined with the Wachovia National Bank to become the Wachovia Bank and Trust Company (now called Wells Fargo). This bank became one of the largest in the South. It was the largest bank between Washington D.C. and Atlanta for many years. He had highly successful branches in Asheville, Salisbury, Spencer, and High Point. Fries remained president until his death.

Henry E. Fries was also president of the Home Moravian Church Sunday School, founder of Washington Cotton Mills, located in Fries, Virginia, and founder of the Mayodan Moravian Church in Mayodan, NC.

The arch over the Fries Family mausoleum at Salem City Cemetery.

The Fries Family mausoleum in Salem Cemetery, Winston-Salem, NC.

Mount Airy Granite mausoleums located in the Salem City Cemetery, Winston- Salem, NC.

4. **Charles Keesee (Oct. 26, 1861-February 18, 1940)**

Last, but certainly not least, Charles Keesee was a banker from Martinsville, Virginia that also owned one quarter of the quarry with Col. Fries and William Shaffner and Mr. Sargent. He was the president of Peoples Bank in Martinsville and it was built with Mount Airy Granite.

Peoples Bank in 2011, located on the square in Martinsville, Virginia.

Charels B. Keesee Portrait

Interment Here

Funeral services for Charles Blackwell Keesee, 79 year-old pioneer Martinsville banker and business leader, who died in Lewis-Gale hospital, Roanoke, yesterday morning after a brief illness (of the heart) were conducted at the residence on Church Street here this afternoon at 2:30 o'clock. His pastor, Dr. J. P. McCabe of the First Baptist Church, was in charge, interment followed Oakwood Cemetery.

Active pallbearers were J. Conrad Kearfott, O. D. Ford, R. P. Gravely, J. Clyde Hooker, Dr. E. M. McDaniel, W. R. Broaddus, Jr., Emmett A. Stover and Pannill Rucker, Jr.

Honorary pallbearers were deacons of the First Baptist church members of the board of directors of the various industrial and business enterprises on which the deceased had served.

Born in North Carolina

Mr. Keesee was the youngest son of Captain John Dupuy Keesee and Jane Johnston Keesee. He was born at the ancestral home, Oak Lawn, in Caswell County, North Carolina on October 26, 1861. He was educated with the other boys in the neighborhood by a private tutor and attended Hall Academy Reidsville, N.C., and Poughkeepsie College, New York. He entered business in Danville, Virginia, when quite a young man and a few years later he located in Martinsville, since which time he has been one of the outstanding citizens of the town and county.

Furniture Pioneer

Mr. Keesee was first engaged in the tobacco manufacturing industry in Martinsville. Subsequently, he was associated with the late A. D. Witten and S. S. Stephen and as the principal organizers of the American Furniture Company. He has been one of the leaders in all of the other industries in this section of the state and has served as a director on practically all of the directorates of the city and county. He was also one of the owners of the Granite Company of Mount Airy, N.C. Although Mr. Keesee's business connections were many and diversified, his main interest and inclinations were those of a banker (People's Bank).

Active in Church Work

Mr. Keesee was always interested in all phases of religious work of the community. He was an active and loyal member of the First Baptist church during his entire residence in

Martinsville, serving as a deacon and trustee for many years. He was a Son of the American Revolution and a member of the Society of the Cincinnati. (He may also have been a member of the Rotary Club. His pastor was a member and also his Mount Airy Granite business partners.)

Mr. Keesee is survived by his widow who was Miss Olivia Helms Simmons, of Floyd County, and the following nieces and nephews: Mrs. A. K. Walker and Miss Janie and Ruth Rawley, all of Reidsville, N.C., Mrs. R. A. Stokes, of Ruffin, N. C.; Ernest Rawley, of Pelham, N.C., and John D. Rawley, of St. Paul, Minnesota.

Kessee – Simmons Mount Airy Granite Mausoluem, Martinsville, Virginia.

    Further research revealed that Mr. Keesee had a talent in business for getting to the heart of a problem. One person said that he was "an embodiment of the American virtues of hard work, thriftiness, and frugality."

    Mr. Keesee was the president of the Peoples's Bank in Martinsville. It was constructed with ashlar cut stone from North Carolina Granite. It is a very unique, castle looking building on the main square.

Upon his and Mrs. Keesee's deaths, a foundation was formed called the Charles B. Keesee foundation that was to be used for the education of Baptist children in the state of Virginia. Sadly the Keesees never had children of their own thus their whole estate went to the foundation. Their home was left for the First Baptist Church of Martinsville for use as a parsonage.

It is important to note that without the financial backing of these four men, Sargent, Shaffner, Fries, and Keesee, the granite quarry would more than likely have stalled out in the Great Depression. Due to their astute business sense and advertising campaign, the company expanded and grew.

Other Notable Mausoleums:

Dodge Brothers Mausoleum in Detroit, Michigan

John Francis Dodge and Horace Dodge were brothers that founded the automobile company called "Dodge Brothers" in Detroit, Michigan. They were inseparable as children and as adults. John was the sales manager type and Horace was the mechanic type. Together they had the makings of a two man operation.

In early 1920, Horace Dodge, one of the famous Dodge brothers contracted the Spanish flu and pneumonia while in New York. He died on January 14, 1920 and his body was interred in the Egyptian style mausoleum with the two Sphinx heads located in Woodlawn Cemetery in Detroit. The following year his brother died and the widows sold the automobile company.

The sphinxes carved for their monument was taken on parade in Mount Airy before being shipped to Detroit. The Museum of Regional History in Mount Airy has a photo of the parade on display.

Early photo of the Dodge Brothers Mausoleum.

Photo of the Sphynxes on the Dodge Brothers Mausoleum, Feb. 4, 2007.
Courtesy of Einar Einarsson Kvaran

2011 Photos of the Dodge Brothers Mausoleum.
Courtesy of Michael Hojnacki

Vahalla Mausoleum, Saint Louis, Missouri is very large and holds several hundred crypts.

This mausoleum is located in Oakwood Cemetery, High Point, NC.

Sylvania Mausoleum in Ohio. Public Domain Photo

To see photos of this mausoleum up close go to www.toledomemorialpark.com. They call it the Swan Lake Mausoleum and Chapel and it is located in Sylvania, Ohio. The interior boast an indoor chapel called the Chapel of Peace.

The Tomb of Ulysses S. Grant

General Grant National Memorial, Grant's Tomb (Mausoleum), as seen in this vintage postcard.

The tomb of Ulysses S. Grant is the largest personal mausoleum in the United States and is located in Manhattan, in River Side Park overlooking the Hudson River. The bodies of Grant (1822– 1885) and his wife, Julia Dent Grant (1826–1902) are interred here.

A groundbreaking ceremony was held on April 27, 1891. John T. Brady was the contractor hired to do the work. Due to a masons strike, construction was delayed and not completed until 1896. It was completed in time for Grant's 75th birthday anniversary, April 27, 1897. One million New Yorkers and 60,000 military soldiers turned out for the ceremony. A very prestigious competition was held throughout the U.S. for a design. The winner of the contest was an architect named John Hemenway Duncan. Duncan was one of sixty-five contestants. He specifically designed the tomb to show respect to a military veteran and not a home.

The tomb went through much decay and neglect over the years. In the mid 1990's a descendant went to the park authorities and threatened to have Grant's body returned to his home state if the tomb was not repaired. Once it was repaired a rededication ceremony was conducted on April 27, 1997.

U.S. Grant in the Civil War 1861-1865

Dedication of Grant's Tomb on April 27, 1897. It is estimated that 1.5 million New Yorkers attended Grants funeral procession.

Ulysses S. Grant tomb September 16, 2004. Courtesy of D. Schwen

Wyatt Jackson Armfield Maousoleum

Wyatt Jackson Armfield of High Point, North Carolina, was a very successful banker. He was the founder of ten banks in the Piedmont region of North Carolina. He was born on November 26, 1843 and died October 12, 1933. He was also one of the first one hundred shareholders in the Guilford Battleground Company.

W.J. Armfield mausoleum in Oakwood Cemetery

W. J. ARMFIELD DIES; WELL KNOWN BANKER

Founded Ten Different Institutions In Piedmont Area. Retired 25 Years Ago.

NATIVE OF HIGH POINT

Greensboro Daily News Bureau
105 East Broad Street, Phone 2613

High Point, Oct. 12.—Wyatt J. Armfield, pioneer Guilford county banker and business man, died this afternoon at 2 o'clock at his home on West Broad street, a month before his 93d birthday. He had been confined to his bed with a lingering illness since May of this year.

Until his retirement from banking in 1907 his interests were more widely scattered than most North Carolinians. He founded and operated 10 banks which were an important part of industrialization of the piedmont section. In 1876 he and his associates organized the First National bank, of Greensboro, and just 10 years later founded the First National bank, of High Point. He and his late son, Eugene M. Armfield, founded eight other banks in Guilford, Randolph, Davie, Montgomery, Rockingham and Alamance counties. He directed the erection of High Point's first "tall building," the five-story structure, now housing the Wachovia Bank and Trust company. It was the home of the North Carolina Savings Bank and Trust company and later the Bank of Commerce.

Mr. Armfield was born on the old plantation four miles north of here that has been in the hands of his family since 1795. He attended school at the famed Nereus Mendenhall's academy and was at Oak Ridge institute when the war between the states began. He was in the quartermaster's corps of the Confederate army, and was detailed to service in the Mendenhall and McRae woolen mill at Jamestown which was burned by Stoneman's raiders. Mr. Armfield was held captive for a few hours.

For a while Mr. Armfield was engaged in business in the western part of the United States and while there was married to Miss Jennie Britt, who preceded him in death.

He is survived by two daughters, Mrs. R. T. Pickens, Sr., who lived with him; Mrs. Frank Armfield, of Concord; three sons, William J. Armfield, Jr., of Asheboro; W. Frank Armfield, of High Point; Jesse L. Armfield, of Evansville, Ind.; a sister, Mrs. Mary A. White, of the Deep River community. There are 23 grandchildren and two great-grandchildren.

Funeral service will be held from the home on West Broad street Saturday afternoon at 3 o'clock. Service will be conducted by Rev. J. N. Hillard and Rev. George H. Crowell. Interment will take place in the Armfield mausoleum in Oak Wood cemetery.

Roach Family Mausoleum in Reidsville, NC

This mausoleum in Greenview Cemetery in Reidsville, NC belongs to John Alexander "Jack" Roach and his wife Rhoda E. McMichael Roach, parents of William Martin Roach.

Penn Family Mausoleum found in Reidsville, NC

The Penn Family Mausoleum can be found in Greenview Cemetery in Reidsville, NC is the mausoleum to members of the Frank Penn Family. He was the founder of Penn Tobacco that became the American Tobacco Company. Frank's son, Jeff Penn, was the owner of Chinqua Penn Plantation.

Charles W. Fulton Mausoleum Oakdale Cemetery Mt. Airy

Dr. Banner's Mausoleum Oakdale Cemetery Mount Airy

Columns

This beautiful column found on the Penn Mausoleum has carved peacocks and pampas grass carved on the top.

Dedicated to Albert Dabney Shelton (July 4, 1875 – February 14, 1925) of Guilford County, North Carolina, this monument was erected by the employees and associates of the Southern Railway System in Green Hill Cemetery.

CHAPTER 9

GRANITE CHURCHES

Nowhere in the United States will you find a city with as many Mount Airy Granite Churches. They were built with a very distinct craftsmanship that is only found in this little city.

Like the rock they are made of, these churches have stood the test of time and are consecrated by God to minister to the people of Mount Airy. Over the years storms have damaged some of them but they have been repaired and thrive today showing the endurance and faith of the local congregations.

Vintage postcard that shows three of the granite churches in Mount Airy; top left, First Presbyterian (1907-1914), First Baptist (1906), Friends (1904), and the Old Central United Methodist (1895). Courtesy of the Surry County Historical Society Minick Collection

First Baptist Church of Mount Airy

Organized on May 1879 on North Main Street, it was called the Mount Airy Baptist Church of Christ. The charter members numbered 16. Currently the membership is around 800 members.

Work began on the granite structure in 1906. The materials were donated by the Mount Airy Granite Company which was operated by Thomas Woodroffe's children. He died in 1900 and left it in his will for them to donate the granite. Today, that section of the building is used as the "most beautiful fellowship hall" in North Carolina (see old postcard below). Construction was completed in 1912. This building was used for everything until the dedication of the new section May 16, 1953. That section today houses the day care and educational classrooms. A new sanctuary was built and dedicated on October 6, 1968.

The church celebrated their 125 years in 2004. In that time it has grown spiritually as well. Stained glass windows were installed in the old sanctuary when it was built. One unique round stain glassed window makes it stand out from all of the others in Mount Airy.

Three of the stained glass windows found in the first sanctuary of First Baptist Church.

Vintage postcard that was mailed to Jack Sargent's father from Jack's wife, Flora, in 1914.

First Baptist, North Main Street, Mount Airy, in 2011.

Trinity Episcopal

In the spring of 1896, construction began on the current building of Trinity Episcopal Church of Mount Airy. Tesh Construction is listed as the contractor for the building in the National Register Historic Places. The first service was held in July of 1896. It was consecrated on October 13, 1900. It was dedicated to " ...the Worship and Service of Almighty God, the administration of His Holy Sacraments, the Reading and Preaching of His Holy Word, and for the performance of All Holy Offices."

JEB Stuart's family attended this church.

One of the most unique items in this church is one of the baptistery bowls. It is also carved from Mount Airy Granite.

In 1954 and addition was made that included offices and Sunday school rooms.

Trinity Episcopal Church, Main Street, Mount Airy, NC

A pile of rocks ceases to be a rock when somebody contemplates it with the idea of a cathedral in mind. – Antoine de Saint-Exupery

Mount Airy Friends

The Religious Society of Friends was composed of religious organizations that arose out of a Christian movement in the 17th Century England. This movement focused on the average individuals' relationship with Christ. They were led by over 50 itinerant preachers known as the Valiant Sixty, including James Naylor, George Fox, Margaret Fell and Francis Howgill. During the 19th and 20th centuries, various splits occurred within the Friends organization.

Friends are well known for testifying about their faith by their actions and how they live their lives. In the mid-nineteenth century they wore a simple form of dress and addressed each other with a simple form of address of "Thee and Thou." They are considered one of the Peace Churches along with the Church of the Brethren.

Established in 1898, the Friends Church of Mount Airy erected the current building on South Main Street in 1904. It is listed on the National Register Historic places. This church has a distinguished bell tower.

Mount Airy Friends Church, South Main Street, Mount Airy, NC

First Presbyterian Church of Mount Airy

Located on South Main Street, the First Presbyterian Church of Mount Airy boast two beautiful red doors that contrast with the Mount Airy Granite. Erected between 1907 and 1914, First Presbyterian Church has maintained a very devoted congregation focused on service.

First Presbyterian Church on South Main Street, Mount Airy, NC

Finding its origins in Scotland, the Presbyterian Church came out of the protestant reformation of the 16th Century. The first Presbyterian Church was founded in Pennsylvania in the 1700's. The first presbytery, organized by four immigrant Irish and Scottish Reformed Presbyterian ministers, was not formed until 1774. The Presbyterians were mostly concentrated in eastern Pennsylvania and northern South Carolina, at this time, but small groups of Reformed Presbyterians existed in Massachusetts, Connecticut, New York, western Pennsylvania, North Carolina, and Georgia. During the American Revolution, most Presbyterians fought for independence, the one minister that served in South Carolina was even arrested for insurrection and brought before Lord Cornwallis in 1780. They were against slavery and fought for the Union in the Civil War, thus
closing many of the established churches in the south.

The front of the First Presbyterian Church of Mount Airy

Zion Baptist Church

Zion Baptist Church of Mount Airy, NC

Zion Baptist Church, Virginia Street, Mount Airy., built ca. 1895. Information on the back of this photo reads, "Zion Baptist Church as it stood on the old Virginia Street. Members of the congregation pose with their guests." A listing of members and unknown guests was written on the back of the picture : "1st row left to right: Will Tucker, Rev. Sloan, Dave Poid, unknown (brother of
Mr. S. Leonard), unknown, unknown, Sonny Leonard, Julia Leonard, Charlie Valentine, J. R. Mathis; 2nd row left to right: unknown, unknown, Miss. Nell Hughes, Josh Hubbard, unknown, unknown, Mrs. Ellen Hines, Miss Mozell Mathis, unknown, Mrs. Lillie Bunker, Mrs. Mary Cockerham (unidentified Piet), Mrs. Sarah Leonard (holding Sonny Tucker); back row unknown, Christina Farrell, Mrs. Farrell, unknown, Martha Conrad, Mrs. Nora Glover." Courtesy of the Surry County Historical Society Minick Collection

Flat Rock Presbyterian Church

Located on Quarry Road at the entrance to North Carolina Granite Corporation, this church was built with volunteer labor around 1903, with granite that was quarried just a few feet away. This building contains many stained windows donated by members that include former employees of the quarry.

The Church of Scotland is the Presbyterian Church. The roots of this church can be traced back to 1560 when the earliest christians were known to be in Scotland. In 1560 teh Scottish Parliment abolished papal jurisdiction and approved John Calvin's confession of Faith, but did not accept many of the principles laid out in John Knox's *First Book of Discipline,* which argued, among other things that all the assets of the old church should pass to the new. In 1560 Reformaitoin Settlement was not ratified by the crown for some years. In 1572 the acts fo 1560 were approved by the young James VI. More theological history of the Presbyterian church exist. It is too much for this book.

Flat Rock Presbyterian started as a mission church in the old Flat Rock School house. I imagine that it also held meetings in the cabin on the Marshall farm to start. The cornerstone was laid on September 12, 1903. Land was donated by the Gilmer family to use forever. If by some chance the church disbanded then the land would go back to the heirs. Currently the land has the church, parsonage, and two other buildings.

In the early days of the quarry, stonecutters were recruited from Scotland, Italy, France, and Czechoslovakia. Many answered the call to Mount Airy. The Scottish stonecutters primarily were the builders and members of the Flat Rock Presbyterian Church. The Thompson House where most of them lived is within site of the church.

Granite was brought up to the site from the quarry. The cutters set to work with hand patent brushes and striking hammers, folding rule, steel square, chalk, plumb, straight edges, and other chisel tools carving the blocks for the church. With these seemingly crude tools, the workers were capable of cutting very small tolerances.

Every state in the Union has scottish stone cutter stories and this is one of Mount Airy's many. When other stone cutters would strike the scottish would work. In the 1880's during many strikes, scottish stone cutters filled the gaps.

Flat Rock Presbyterian Church (now and then) built in 1903.

Flat Rock Presbyterian Church then photo.

Grace Moravian Church of Mount Airy

Grace Moravian Church traces its roots to 1923 when Brother Charles D. Crouch began having services. Early services were held at town hall, store buildings, and possible other gathering places in Mount Airy. On March 15, 1925, ninety- six people were baptized and accepted into the church. On September 13, 1925, the cornerstone was laid for the new church building.

In 1924, land was acquired for the parsonage to be built on West Elm Street.

The Sunday School was built in 1955 and the sanctuary was renovated in 1962. In 1965, another addition was planned including the steeple. At this time the steeple was placed on the building.

Grace Moravian Church located on North Main Street, Mount Airy, North Carolina.

Flat Rock Baptist Church of Mount Airy

In 1875 John Bower built a log cabin church somewhere on the Marshall Farm. This was bout one and one half miles from the crossroads in Flat Rock. Several denominations used the facility for their worship services until they could get established.

The Flat Rock Baptist Church is located on 103 just two miles east of Mount Airy. Originally it was organized at Laurel Hill on January 15, 1899 with the help of the First Baptist Church of Mount Airy. Services were held in the Flat Rock Elementary School until 1905 when they erected a building just for church services, also built with Mount Airy Granite. Dr. Reverand C.C. Haymore oversaw the organization of the church and Brother J. W. Simmons named the church. The first minister was J. H. Powers. In 1911 Reverand Haymore served as pastor.

The church remodeled the old Flat Rock School in 1907. The county had ideas of how the school should look but the parents did not like the plans so they rallied together and designed the school themselves. They pulled together and provided the materials, including the granite, for a very unique and beautiful learning environment. It was covered in what is called "One and Two Man Rubble" (same as retaining wall blocks). Once finished they were very proud of their product.

I found this quote about the school.

"Generations may come and go; the roof and subsequent roofs may rot and fall; even the worn and much be whittled benches may be many times replaced but those sturdy walls of "Mount Airy – the Whitest Granite" will stand forever as an endearing monument to the intelligence and farsightedness of those builders, who while they are building, built **Once and Forever**."

In 1937, Flat Rock Baptist Church bought the old school building and converted it into a working church. In 1954 they built the educational wing.

In 1974 after years of growth the church contracted to build a new sanctuary. Later in 1998 it was remodeled.

Holy Angels Catholic Church, Mount Airy, NC

Established in 1921, the Holy Angels Catholic Church is built with Mount Airy Granite and located on North Main Street.

More Granite Churches

Church of the Holy Comforter, Burlington, NC

Lawrence Shackelford Holt handed over the deed on November 5, 1911 as he stood before the congregation. He did this along with his wife, Margaret Locke Erwin Holt, in memory of their beautiful young daughter, Emily Holt. His one requirement was the pews never be sold and that the members would always own the church. The congregation is very diverse and today has over 500 members from Greensboro to Raleigh that attend Sunday morning service. It is called the Holy Comforter because the Holts said that during their time of sadness their greatest comfort came from the church.

Located in downtown Burlington amongst a beautiful green grove of trees, the Saint Anthansius Church, built in 1880, sits behind the building. This quaint little church served the congregation well but they outgrew it and the Holt family graciously contributed to the building of the current gothic style sanctuary. They also commissioned a stained glass window to overshadow the altar.

Episcopal Church of the Holy Comforter, Burlington, North Carolina

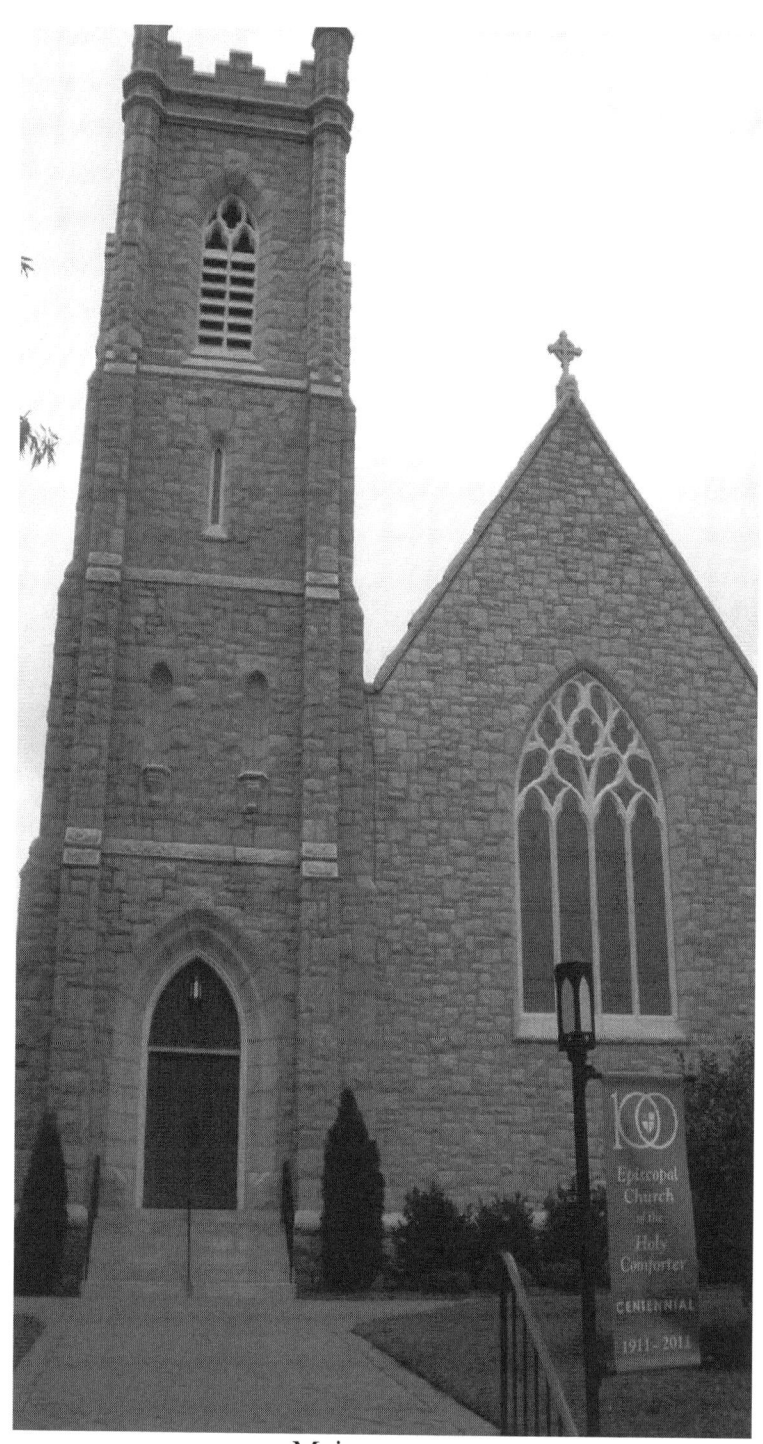

Main entrance

Central United Methodist Church (Salisbury, NC)

The Central United Methodist Church, Salisbury, NC has a Mount Airy Granite foundation.

St. Margaret's Roman Catholic Church (Lancaster, PA)

Ritcher & Eiler, Architect of Reading, Pennsylvania designed the church building. Reider & McLaughlin conducted the general contract work and the masonry.

Formerly the Zion Reformed Church (Baltimore, MD), now called the Shepherd Community Baptist Church.

Located at the intersection of Harford Road and Iona Avenue, this church was designed by Frederick Thomas, Architect, and built by John J. Kelly, general contractor of Baltimore. Seymour Ruff & Sons of Baltimore did the masonry work.

Zion Baptist Today

Bethesda M.E. Church (Salisbury, MD)

George Savage, Archictect, from Philadelphia, designed this beautiful church. The general contractor was Hastings & Parsons of Salisbury, Maryland. Seymour Ruff & Sons of Baltimore, Maryland did the masonry.

Rectory of Holy Child Roman Catholic Church (Philadelphia, PA)

This beautiful church was built at the intersection of Broad and Duncannon Streets in Philadelphia by McLaughlin & McNally, General Contractors. It was designed by G. I. Lovatt, Architect of Allentown, PA. Luigi Rosmini supervised the masonry work.

St. Charles Borromeo Seminary Group (Overbrook, PA)

Architect Paul Monaghan of Philadelphia designed this large seminary group. It was constructed by the general contractor, McCloskey & Company. Tony Kennedy & Sons did the masonry work.

St. Charles was founded in 1832 by the most Reverend Francis P. Kenrick of Philadelphia. Chartered in 1838 to grant degrees, St. Charles Brrromeo Seminary is commissioned on Higher Education of the Middle States Association of Colleges and Schools, and the Association of Theological Schools of the United States and Canada. This is a Catholic preparatory school and seminary.

The buildings in this photo were constructed in the 1870's.

CHAPTER 10

GRANITE HOMES

The landscapes of North Carolina towns are dotted with homes built of North Carolina granite. Mount Airy has the largest number of these homes with Greensboro next in the numbers. Gracious beautiful homes are in both cities. Typically built in the 1920's, these homes were owned by successful business men.

This chapter is very important because of the splendid architecture of a granite home is the reason this book was written. Although some are similar, no two are the same and once a home is built with granite, with the right care, they can last forever.

A common thread that you will discover in North Carolina is the work of Architect Harry Barton (June 17, 1876-May 9, 1937). Mr. Barton was a native of Pennsylvania. He moved to Greensboro, North Carolina around 1912 to join Frank A. Weston in business. Thus began his leadership career in the architectural industry. He took an active role in the American Institute of Architects in North Carolina and held office for several years.

Harry attended two different universities, Temple College and George Washington University. Later he studied at the Beaux Arts Institute of Design. Before moving to North Carolina he worked in Philadelphia and Washington D.C. for the Office of the Supervising Architect, United States Department of Treasury, designing federal buildings primarily in the Midwest. It is unknown to the author at this time if he used Mount Airy Granite in any of the western buildings, but it is noted that there are several buildings in D.C. built with Mount Airy Granite.

Homes of Granite in Mount Airy, Proper

J. H. Hadley Home (Built in 1899)

This is the first home built of granite in Mount Airy, ca. 1899. Granite was quarried from the site and used directly in the construction.

The lovely Queen Anne style home was the home of J. H. Hadley, a very successful tobacco manufacturer in Mount Airy. He held the office of Mayor at one point and owned a cotton mill in Siler City. Today this home is listed on the National Register of Historic Places.

J. D. "Jack" Sargent Home (1919, Mount Airy, NC)

This impressive granite and timber bungalow represents the success of Mr. Jack Sargent (1871 - 1945), former respected President of the North Carolina Granite Corporation. The walls are both rusticated and ashlar cut stone, very large stone porch posts, stone chimneys, a cut stone balustrade, yard ornaments, and stone terrace. Also, a beautiful stone garage stands behind the house. Influenced by the Tudor-Revival style, the house has "half - timbered" gables and dormer windows and a tile roof. The interior is of the Craftsman style with a granite fireplace and a granite mantle. The decorative hardwood floors have inlaid wood designs, walls surrounded by high-paneled wainscoting. The dining room is particularly beautiful due to this feature. It is, also, on the National Register of Historic Places.

Mr. Sargent worked as a superintendent for a few companies in Vermont before moving to Mount Airy and becoming the superintendent of the Granite Quarry in 1910. In 1918, Mr. Sargent bought the company and served for the remainder of his life as the President. He is recognized as the one that built the company to the national level that it is known today.

The Jack Sargent house on Main Street, Mount Airy, NC.

Raymond Sargent Home (1927, Mount Airy, NC)

Like his father's home, Raymond Sargent's home is also a bungalow style in one-and-a-half stories. This house contains broad, bracketed gables and a nice granite porch, side chimney, and a terrace.

He was born in North Jay, Franklin County, Maine on 1895. He was the Son of John Davis "Jack" Sargent and Flora Kimball Sargent.

Obituary in the Mt. Airy News, November 10, 1964.

Funeral services for John Raymond Sargent, 69 of Dallas, Texas, were conducted at 10am Friday at Restland Memorial Chapel there by the Rev. Thomas J. Shipp. Burial was in Restland Memorial Park. Sargent died Wednesday morning in a Dallas hospital after a long illness. He was born in North Jay, Maine and had lived in Mount Airy several years before moving to Texas 20 years ago. he was the son of the late Mr. and Mrs. J.D. Sargent of Mount Airy. He was employed by Temco (Timco) as an aircraft inspector until his retirement five years ago. He was a veteran of World War I, and a member of John L DeGrazier Masonic Lodge, Dallas Commandery No. 6 and Hella Temple. He was a member of Lakewood Methodist Church.
Surviving are his wife; two daughters, Mrs. Elizabeth Cothran of Florence, S.C. and Miss Pollyanna Sargent of Washington, D.C.; three grandchildren; and a sister Mrs. Ruth Sargent Martin of Mount Airy.

George D. Fawcett Home (1910)

Built with North Carolina Granite, the George D. Fawcett home is a two- story Colonial Revival style with a fairly simple, but grand, sturdy, design. It contains a hipped roof, a wraparound porch, and a front entrance with side lights. The entrance is a "pedimented entrance bay" and has a projecting pavilion on the southeast corner. Mr. Fawcett was President of the First National Bank, following in his father's footsteps. He was then succeeded by his brother, Garnett Fawcett as president of the First National Bank in 1920, following his death. Their homes are located side by side on Main Street.

George D. Fawcett Home on Main Street, Mount Airy, NC

T. Garnett Fawcett Home (1905-1910)

Thomas Garnett Fawcett was a cashier at two banks, First National Bank (that his father, Thomas, founded and his brother, George, was president) and at Surry County Loan and Trust Company. After his brother, George Fawcett passed away in 1920, Garnett became president of First National Bank. This home is also two-story and a granite Colonial Revival style. It features a hipped roof with intersecting shingled gables. The dormers are pedimented. It contains a wraparound porch with Doric columns, plain balustrade, and a pedimented entrance similar to his brother's home next door.

John Springthorpe Home (1930's)

John Springthorpe was the founder of Pine State Knitwear. He had this home built in the 1930's in the Chateauesque (Castle) style. It is two-storied and stuccoed on the upper portion with most of the home being built with granite. The towered entrance has a polygonal roof.

Springthorpe home, Mount Airy, NC

John Prather Frank Home (1940's)

John Prather Frank succeeded Jack Sargent as President of the North Carolina Granite Corporation in 1945. The beloved Mr. Frank was the longest serving president of the company when he retired in 1977 with a total of 45 years of service. His employees remembered him as a great boss that cared about his employees and their families. He was involved in the community through his church and the Rotary Club of Mount Airy. Mr. Frank's home was built in the 1940's as a cottage style. Later he had the front faced with granite.

John Prather Frank home, Mount Airy, NC

Sam Hennis House (1923)

The Sam Hennis home is a fantastic example of the bungalow style. A long granite drive way leads the visitor up to the home. It is one-and-one-half story house constructed with native Mount Airy granite for the first story, porch, and chimneys. The central part, upper story, and broad gables are stuccoed. The porch is offset and contains a side porte-cochere, low rooflines, large overhanging eves, and windows in groups of threes.

Stephen "Steve" Mason Hale Home (Built sometime after 1900)

The Stephen M. Hale home was located where the BB & T now stands in Mount Airy. The photograph shows ornate gingerbread detail along the eves of the front porch. It is possible that it was designed by Architect Harry Barton because it is very similar to some of this other designs.

Mr. Hale was born in Oldtown, Grayson County, Virginia on January 28, 1862. At the age of 19 he married Emma Cooper from Wythe County, Virginia. They were married on October 5, 1882.

Mr. Hale was educated at the Old Elk Creek Academy and clerked in stores throughout the community. He went into business for himself in Ennis in 1888 and remained there for 11 years. Hauling his merchandise from Mount Airy to Ennis over the rough and rugged mountains was very strenuous for Mr. Hale.

In 1899, Mr. Hale moved his business to Mount Airy where for 40 years he operated Hale's Department Store on Main Street. Mr. Hale died on May 16, 1942 very suddenly at his home in Mount Airy. He was the last remaining of 12 children of Wiley D. Hale and Martha Grayson Mitchell Hale.

S. M. Hale Clothing Store, formerly located on Main Street in Mount Airy. S. M. Hale and Will Hale in doorway flanked by two employees (unknown). Currently Holcomb Hardware. Courtesy of the Surry County Historical Society

Stephen M. Hale grave granite marker located in the Oakdale Cemetery Mount Airy, NC.

More Granite Homes

Granite cottage, Mount Airy, NC

Mount Airy FRIENDS parsonage.

This home with three granite chimneys is located on the North Carolina Granite Quarry property and was a rental home for employees of the quarry in the past.

Greensboro and Winston-Salem, North Carolina Homes

John Marion "J.M." Galloway House (1919)

Located at 1007 Elm Street in Greensboro, this home is another Harry Barton project that was completed in 1919 for J. M. Galloway. It is a magnificent example of a cross between craftsman and gothic architecture with large wooden beams and ashler cut stone. Mr. Galloway made his career as a tobacco broker and he was originally from Stokes County, North Carolina. He was a veteran of the Civil War. His home is my personal favorite of all the granite homes I have discovered.

J.M.'s tombstone in Green Hill Cemetery

The J.M. Galloway home THEN and NOW.

Residence of Mr. A. M. Galloway, Greensboro, N. C. Mr. Harry Barton, Architect

Granite for the House Beautiful

GRANITE is one of the most beautiful and durable materials for the exterior of the country house or city residence. Variety of color and texture and the many interesting methods of jointing and finish provide the architect with a material of exceptional adaptability.

The residence illustrated above is a pleasing example of irregularly jointed "broken range" granite ashler with rough hewn sills and arch stones, hammer dressed steps, cap stones and urns. In addition to its unsurpassed durability and weather resisting qualities, granite walls have the paradoxical qualities of keeping a house cool in summer and warm in winter.

For landscape features, entrance gateways, walls, curbs and steps, granite has unquestionable qualifications combining beauty and harmony with permanence.

National Building Granite Quarries Association, Inc.

H. H. Sherman, *Secretary*   51 State Street, Boston, Mass.

"The Noblest of Building Stone"

Early advertisement in an Agriculture Magazine.

Fisher Park (1902)

Named for Captain John Basil Fisher, Fisher Park is a residential neighborhood that he donated to the city of Greensboro. He was born in Scotland, a former British Naval Officer, and immigrated to America where he settled in Asheboro. He owned and operated a gold mine. Being unsuccessful in the gold business, he turned to purchasing real estate. The land he purchased in Greensboro is known as Lindsay's Woods. This basically was the trash dump of Greensboro.

In 1902 he donated the land to the city on the condition that they would build a driveway. The streets that they first built for the residential neighborhood are Fisher Park Circle, North Park Drive, and South Park Drive. All of the signs and curbing and bridges for this park that is located in the center of each of these streets, is built with Mount Airy Granite.

Sadly he died shortly thereafter, 1903, in New York. Later his wife had his body reinterred in Green Hill Cemetery near the Wharton Street Entrance.

Several years later two business men of Greensboro started the development and they were Mr. Wharton and Mr. James E. Latham (also buried in Green Hill Cemetery). The neighborhood was developed in stages with the oldest being in 1915.

Bridge wall in Fisher Park

1920's Cottage

Built in the 1920's, this home of Mount Airy Granite is located in Forsyth County.

Granite home, Winston-Salem, NC

Granite cottage, Dobson, NC

"And now here is my secret, a very simple secret; it is only with the heart that one can see rightly, what is essential is invisible to the eye."

~ Antoine de Saint-Exupery

Andrew J. Schlosser (1919)

This very nice Bungalow home was built for Andrew J. Schlosser between 1919 and 1922. Mr. Schlosser's family immigrated from either Germany or Austria. He was a meat packer. His son, Andrew L. Schlosser was a well known architect/engineer in Greensboro that built many of the historic homes.

Behind the home, which is now an office, is a 2 bay garage with tile roofing, also converted into office space. A one car garage was built on the side in 1922. Two chimneys that reach two stories are on each side of the home. A small vestibule was added to the front door at a later date.

Andrew J. Schlosser home photographed in 2011.

Joseph Archie Cannon (1926)

Joseph Archie Cannon (1909-1973) was an attorney in Greensboro. His home sits on a hill with a set of granite steps leading up to the front porch. The house has a beautiful patio and front porch. It has a nice granite fireplace in the front sitting room. Behind the home is a garage that matches the house with a tile roof. The home's screened in porch on the right and sunroom on the left has railing around the roof.

Mount Airy Granite steps leading up to the Cannon home onWest Market Street, Greensboro, NC.

James E. Latham (1913)

Mr. Latham was the President of Pomona Cotton Mills and J. E. Latham Real Estate Company. He was also the Vice President of Atlantic Bank and Trust Company, Greensboro Warehouse and Storage Company, and Chairman of the board of the Jefferson Standard Life Insurance Company. His home has been converted into condos and is very large. Wells L. Brewer built this home in 1913 for Mr. Latham. Latham died on April 16, 1946.

Early photo of the J. E. Latham home.

James E. Latham home on Fisher Park Circle in Greensboro, NC.

Dr. Charles Whitlock Banner (N. Elm Street)

Dr. Banner's home was located on North Elm Street in Greensboro. His office was about 1 mile down the street in the heart of the city in the Banner Building. His home no longer exists but as you can see from this photo it was a fine granite home on a hill. All that exists today are the steps and retaining walls.

Dr. Banner was born April 29, 1867 in Surry County, North Carolina and died August 30, 1964, at the ripe old age of 97 in Greensboro. His early education was in the public schools of Mount Airy. At the age of 12 he became a clerk for a druggist. He was a dentist and graduated from the Philadelphia School of Dentistry in 1890. At this point he practiced dentistry for 8 years and was president of the North Carolina Dental Society. Not satisfied with this field he took further courses in the medical field and graduated from the Maryland School for Medicine in 1899. He then became an eye, ear, nose, and throat specialist. He traveled to Europe and practiced medicine there also. His passport can be found on Ancestry.com.

In 1915, he was elected a Fellow of the American College of Surgeons. His professional organizations included American Medical Association, the Southern Medical Association, the North Carolina Medical Society, the Guilford County Medical Society and the American

Association for the advancement of Science, and were President of the Eighth District Medical Society of North Carolina.

Dr. Banner was an Army Reserve Veteran of World War I. His draft card said that he was 5' 7" tall and had grey eyes and dark brown hair.

Dr. Banner was one of the founding members of the Greensboro Country Club and was on the board of directors.

He was the son of the late William Martin Banner and Catherine Whitlock Banner. His father, William successfully farmed tobacco in Surry County. His first wife was Josephine Fawcett. She died in 1938. They had a son, Charles Whitlock Banner, Jr.

Upon his death, his body was interred at the Oakdale Cemetery in Mount Airy. He was a upstanding member of the West Market Street Episcopal Church.

Dr. Banner's former home located on North Elm Street, Greensboro, NC. It was razed and now condos stand on this site. The steps and retaining walls remain.

W. D. Rowe Home

W. D. Rowe was the business partner of William Roach and they owned the granite yard in Greensboro. Census records show him living in Danville, VA in the 1920 and 1930 census.

W D. Rowe Company, Inc.

Founded in 1885 by William D. Rowe, W.D. Rowe Company has crafted grave markers for more than 125 years. W. D. was born in Nashville, Tennessee to an Irish Immigrant. His father was listed as a huckster (street vendor) in the early census. Later he took his selling skills, farmed, and sold produce. W.D. learned the art of sales early. I imagine that when he moved to Danville that he found the need for a marble and granite company, organized the company, and began selling grave markers. His early business was located near the courthouse and jail yards. Thus he could provide service to municipal buildings and cut the cost of transport.

At the turn of the century, Mr. Rowe went into business with William Martin Roach of Greensboro, North Carolina. They were brothers-in-law. Mr. Rowe married Roberta Roach, William Roach's sister from Reidsville, North Carolina. Their company was called Rowe and Roach. Mr. Roach died in a work accident while inspecting a granite job in Wilmington, North Carolina. Like W. D. Rowe Company in Danville, the Rowe and Roach Company was located near the courthouse and near the railroad. The Greensboro Courthouse was constructed of Granite and thus the courtyard became known for a time as the "Granite Yard."

Obie Roach, William Roach's brother, was in the quarry business near Danville and more than likely provided local stone for some of the local projects.

The largest monument built by W.D. Rowe and Company as of 1992 stands 10 to 12 feet tall. Their monuments are constructed with marble, granite, and bronze.

E. W. Myers purchased the company in 1924 after W. D.'s retirement. Mr. Myers stayed with the business until his death in 1974. After his death Leland Scearce Edith, and Clinton Emerson purchased the company. Edith Emerson still owns and operates the company today.

W. D. Rowe Monuments truck onsite with stonecutter in the cemetery.

Stephen, stonecutter for W.D. Rowe Company is carving a date in a stone in September 2011.

Obituary of William D. Rowe

William D. Rowe dies in Hospital (Danville Register, Friday, March 29, 1946, page 5-B)

Funeral services to Be Conducted Tomorrow for Well Known Resident

William D. Rowe, founder of the Marble and granite company which bears his name, died at Memorial Hospital last night at 8:30 o'clock after an illness of seven weeks.

He was born in Nashville, Tenn., on September 28, 1864, a son of the late George A. and Susan C. Rowe. He was reared at Morristown, Tenn.

Mr. Rowe came to Danville (on) July 10, 1890, and continued in the marble and granite business for 47 ½ years, retiring January 1, 1937. During that period of time, he became well known throughout Danville and the surrounding area. He had been a member of Mount Vernon Methodist church since July, 1890.

In recent years, he had been forced into a relatively inactive life as his health began to fail.

His first wife, Mrs. Roberta Roach Rowe, died January 18, 1930.

Mr. Rowe is survived by his wife, Mrs. Maggie Carter Rowe, and a daughter by the first marriage, Mrs. Ethel Rowe Bass, Miami, Fla.

Also left are two grandsons, J. Gordon Bass, Jr. of the Air Corps overseas, and William Rowe Bass, Miami Fla., and a brother, Frank R. Rowe, Bedford, Ind.

Funeral services will be conducted Saturday at 11 a.m. from Mount Vernon Methodist church and interment will follow in Mountain View Cemetery.

Homes of Granite in High Point, North Carolina

Dr. Grayson Home (Bernice Bienenstock Furniture Library)

This beautiful granite home was formerly the home of Dr. Charles and Bertha Grayson and is located on Main Street. It was completed in 1925. Dr. Grayson was born in 1875 in McDowell County. He received his education at George Washington University and got his medical degree at 1906.

Built of rock- faced Mount Airy Granite, the Colonial revival house was constructed between 1923 and 1925. The late Harry Barton was the architect. He was French trained in the Beau Arts. Between 1912 and the 1930's he designed many homes and buildings throughout North Carolina.

Dr. Grayson was a well recognized physician in the early part of the twentieth century. It is said that he delivered over 7,600 babies. Dr. Grayson died in 1962. Bertha remained in the home until 1967.

Not only was Dr. Grayson a successful physician, he also served as mayor of High Point for four terms, three terms on city council, and he was deacon of First Baptist Church.

In October of 1994, this home was selected for the National Register of Historic Places. Sadly, it is the only Granite home in High Point still standing. There are others that have a foundation but none that are totally granite. Both of Dr. Grayson's daughters were living at the time of the designation and were thrilled that their childhood home was chosen such an honor.

A most distinctive feature of this house is the roof. It is Ludowici-Celadon red clay tile roof.

The house has a matching garage and like the house it is has a roof in red with straight –barrel mission tiles. Originally, the home had four bedrooms and a sitting room upstairs. The downstairs had a parlor, dining room, small sitting room, and kitchen.

Current history of the home begins in 1968 when N. I. "Sandy" Bienenstock and his wife, Bernice, purchased the home from Bertha Grayson's estate. Sandy's dream was to develop a furniture library that was like no other and comprehensive to the furniture industry. In 1970, the home was opened as a library. It is operated by a non- profit foundation, The Furniture Library Association.

On April 9, 1970, Terry Sanford, then president of Duke University, Durham, North Carolina, dedicated the library in memory of his 1961 running mate, Lt. Gov. H. Cloyd Philpott. Mr. Sanford was introduced by Charles Myers, president of Burlington Industries.

Open the public, the library is home to the largest collection of books and research materials related to the furniture industry. The Bienenstocks had collected furniture books for over 60 years.

Home of Dr. Charles and Mrs. Bertha Grayson, Main Street, High Point, NC.

The student has his Rome, his Florence, his whole glowing Italy, within the four walls of his library. He has in his books the ruins of an antique world and the glories of a modern one. ~Henry Wadsworth Longfellow

Librarian is a service occupation. Gas station attendant of the mind. ~Richard Powers

Dr. Charles Grayson home garage.

On North Main Street in High Point sits this gracious home with a granite foundation and timber structure. It is now an antique shop.

Other Razed Homes

The Frank Wineskie Home was a landmark in High Point. An article in the High Point Enterprise dated July 14, 1967, talks about the quality construction of the home. The reporter said that it was "sturdy as the rock of which it was made and yielded reluctantly to demolition efforts." No expense was spared on the construction of this home, which included solid oak paneling in the living room and halls, while the dining and music rooms were paneled in solid mahogany. The windows were made from beveled plate glass. Snow Lumber Company was the contractor for all of the woodwork. Mr. Wineskie was a pioneer business man and civic leader in High Point. He chaired the Sheraton's building committee and made his fortune with Southern Mirror and Glass, then he turned to a full-fashioned hosiery mill called Diamond Hosiery Mills.

Frank Wineskie organized the first service club of men on his front porch in October of 1919. In 1920, he was a charter member of the High Point Rotary Club International.

The former Wineskie home in High Point, NC.

Ragan Home (no photo)

Another razed home that is no longer standing was the W. P. Ragan home on West High Street. It was used by the Full Gospel Church. This home had a very large veranda porch all the way around and stood three stories.

E. Alexander, scion of a pioneering merchandising family built a granite home to replace his ancestral frame home at English and Elm, just a block north of his brother-in-law, Charles F. Long. It was razed and an office building was built in its place called the Mendenhall-Moore building. Mr. Long's home was similar to Mr. Alexander's in architecture. The Long house was three stories with granite up the first two stories. The yard had a granite fence all around.

Kapp Home

Former Dr. Henry H. Kapp home, Holly Street, Winston-Salem, NC.

Bill Shaffner Home

Former William Bill Shaffner home, North of Old Salem, Winston-Salem, NC.

Granite Homes in Salisbury, North Carolina

Granite bungalow is located in the historic district.

Located in Salisbury, NC, this home has been converted into an office.

This home and carriage house is located in the historic district of Salisbury.

This carriage house sits behind the home on the previous page.

This home is located in the historic district near the rail road.

Granite Homes Found in Reidsville, North Carolina

Wyatt Hearp Home, Reidsville, NC

Built in 1946, this was the home of Wyatt Hearp. It took two years to construct and before it was complete, lightning hit the home and burned a small spot in the rafters before extinguishing. The granite was delivered by train to the Reidsville Depot and then hauled by truck to the site. The home was remodeled in 2002.

The Wyatt Hearp Home in Reidsville, NC.

This is another granite home found in Reidsville proper.

This the side entrance to the Dr. John Hester and Minnie Roach Hester home in Reidsville. The foundation, gate post, and fence post are Mount Airy Granite. She was the sister to William Martin Roach of Greensboro.

Granite homes found in Danville, Virginia

The Peter Booth home is located on West Main Street in Danville, Virginia and has been completely remodeled with eight fireplaces; front porch handrail in photo below.

This home was built from the left over granite used to build the Booth Brothers homes.

Four historic homes located on West Main Street in Danville.

First on the left was built with left over granite from the construction of the last two on the right. Second on the left is a brick home. The Booth Brothers hired this home built. Third home, left to right, is the former home of Peter Booth and remodeled by Susan Stilwell. Fourth home, left to right, is the former Charlie Booth home.

    The last two were contracted by the Booth Brothers, Virginia Bank and Trust founders and grocery store merchants. Four Italian stone masons cut the stone onsite and built the homes. The stonecutters had been working on the dam near Riverside Cotton Mills (Dan River Mills). Five of the original six founders of the Riverside Cotton Mills formed the Dan River Powwer and Manufacturing plant on the Dan River in 1895. They would have needed expert stonemasons to build the dam and construct the power plant. More than likely that is when the Italian stonemasons moved to Danville. Once that was finished they hired themselves out to build these homes. The granite was hauled in by train to the granite yard and then delivered to the site.

Charlie Booth's home, now the Callahan home, West Main St., Danville, VA

Former Governor Montague Home in Danville with granite foundation.

Granite Homes in Burlington, North Carolina

Cottage style homes are located in the Fifth Street Historic District of Burlington, NC.

    The North Fifth Street Historic District of Burlington contains three granite bungalows that were built during the 1920s and 1930s. Three different materials were used in three different style homes. This one shows a gable dormer, granite posts and balustrades, steps and two granite chimneys.

    These homes were built during the golden years of Burlington when textiles were the major economic benefactor. Today the Laboratory Corporation of America fills that niche.

Another cottage located in the historic district of Burlington, NC.

The Former C. Freeman (Diamond Pete) Neese Home

This very unusual granite home was built in 1918 for Harold C. Pollard, realtor. It is located on 728 W. Davis Street. It is located on a corner lot next to the entrance gates to Fountain Place. The gates are also built from Mount Airy Granite. J. W. Long, contractor from Greensboro, won the construction contract to build this home.

During the 1920s, C. Freeman (Diamond Pete) Neese purchased the home. He was the son of C. Freeman Neese, Sr., who opened the very first jewelry store in Burlington during the 1880s.

CHAPTER 11

GRANITE BRIDGES

In the early 1930's, the New Deal was signed into law by then President Franklin D. Roosevelt. As part of the New Deal Package came the Bureau of Public Roads. The very first landscape architect was hired to build an aesthetically pleasing road that became known as the Mount Vernon Memorial Highway. This was not a new idea but definitely was in the peak of being in "style." Several New York Parkways were already constructed using the natural landscape materials. It is no surprise that Mount Airy Granite was one of the desired materials for a beautiful and sturdy bridge.

Here are just a few examples of granite bridges.

Arlington National Bridge (Washington, DC)

This is a vintage linen postcard of the Arlington National Bridge.

More than 300,000 square feet of Mount Airy Granite was used to make this beautiful bridge that crosses the Potomac River near Arlington National Cemetery. The bridge is 2200 feet long and was constructed in 1925.

Bryn Mawr Avenue Bridge (Media, Pennsylvania)

Bryn Mawr Avenue Bridge

Located in Delaware County, Pennsylvania, this bridge was funded by the county commissioners. They liked it so much that others were built.

George Wright was the county engineer at the time of construction for Delaware County, Pennsylvania. McHale & Company were the contractors hired to build the bridge.

East 9th Street Bridge (Chester, PA) (No Photo)

This single arch bridge was built in Chester, Pennsylvania using #1 and #2 Man Rubble. Very similar bridges were built all over the United States but this one was built with Mount Airy Granite. This bridge is still in use today.

George Wright was the county engineer for Delaware County. The general contractor was listed as Carl R. Camp, Inc. of Philadelphia, Pennsylvania. Tony Kennedy and Sons were the masons from Philadelphia that were hired.

Brower Mill Granite Bridge, Mount Airy, North Carolina

Brower Mill Granite Bridge without mortar located on the Old Mill Site in Mount Airy. Courtesy of the Surry County Historical Society

The Brower Mill Bridge is a connection to the past community of Hamburg and the cotton mill, Hambrug Mills. This bridge was built to haul traffic over the mill race. It is believed to be the oldest structure standing built of Mount Airy Granite. Also, it is all that remains of the community built by Jacob Brower in 1841.

     Mr. Brower diverted the Ararat River to run his factories and four mills. The water flowed for about one half mile through the race to the mills. For fifty years, Brower and his sons ran the mills; grinding grain, spinning wool and cotton, making boxes and shoes.

     The local general store was a center for the community where everyone got news and visited their neighbors.

Looking up the stream bed to the bridge.

CHAPTER 12

GRANITE MONUMENTS AND MEMORIALS

Wright Brothers Monument

The idea was formed in the 1927 by the First Flight Society that the first flight of mankind should be commemorated. The First Flight Society formed on August 16, 1927. Construction began with North Carolina Granite in the spring of 1931 and was completed and dedicated on November 19, 1932. A 60 foot tall monument, the largest monument to an individual, was built in honor of the Wright Brothers. This monument is located in Kitty Hawk at Kill Devil Hills, North Carolina. Orville Wright attended the ceremony.

On December 17, 1928, The First Flight Society held the first ceremony commemorating the 25 years since the flight by Orville and Wilbur Right by dedicating a granite boulder at the spot where the plane left the ground. Several of the smaller monuments in this park are also built with Mount Airy Granite. Other granite boulders mark where the plane touched ground.

December 17, 1903, Wilbur and Orville Wright successfully flew for about 2 miles. They achieved a cruising speed of about 30 to 35 miles per hour. They flew about 4 flights that day. Head winds hindered very long flights. (Orville had the mustache.)

On the base of the monument is a reminder to us of the incredible accomplishments of the brothers: *"In commemoration of the conquest of the air by the brothers Wilbur and Orville Wright. Conceived by genius and achieved by dauntless resolution and unconquerable faith."*

Vintage postcards of Wright Brothers Monument, Kitty Hawk, NC

176

A vintage postcard with granite boulder marking flight path of the Wright Brothers Monument

This photo dated 1929 was probably taken shortly after the stone marker was placed at the site of the first flight.

Trenton Battle Monument

The Trenton Battle Monument located in Trenton, New Jersey was designed by John H. Duncan, Architect of President Grant's Tomb. The column of granite is 148 feet high and considered to be a great example of the Beaux Arts style. The column is decorated with acanthus leaves. A ring of stars adorn the crown near the observation platform. Above the platform are 13 lights representing the 13 original colonies. A small statue of George Washington with right arm outreached sits on top. Continental soldiers flank the entrance.

Tombstones

Tombstones have a wide variety of shapes and sizes. The possibilities of design are infinite. Some are a single stone for one person. Others are designed for couples or whole families. In the next section of this book you will see a wide array of tombstones found in the piedmont area of North Carolina that has been discovered in various cemeteries.

This note was found in the New River Notes and is an obituary for Berta Carson.

"There was one daughter, Berta Carson, who was a bright, beautiful girl. She was educated at Mary Baldwin, Staunton, Va., and Hollins Institute. While at Hollins she contracted a cold, which resulted in tuberculosis, from which she suffered three years. And while her family tried every available cure she never recovered, but died in February, 1906, at the age of 22. She was buried in the cemetery at Old Town, Va. A beautiful tombstone of Mount Airy granite with marble slab marks her resting place.

Her mother is devoted to her memory, and keeps fresh flowers on her grave constantly.

When young she joined the Methodist Church at Old Town and lived a devoted Christian life and she rests in peace."

This is the most "comfortable" Mount Airy Granite tombstone and can be found in Oakdale Cemetery.

Tombstone of Dr. Arthur Gates. He practiced general family medicine.

The John Prather Frank Monument in Oakdale Cemetery symbolizes the eternal circle of life and the eternal flame of life.

This is a tombstone for Orizzonte Mastroianni who is buried in Oakdale Cemetery.

The Kochtitzky granite tombstone located in Oakdale Cemetery.

    Caroline Octavia Kochtitzky married William Edward Merritt on 7 June 1893. Ed Merritt founded the W. E. Merritt and Renfro Hosiery Mills companies. Edward Hugh Kochititzky moved to Mount Airy in 1896 from Missouri to become manager of the Mount Airy Furniture Company upon the advice of his brother-in-law, Ed Merritt. He met Alice Sparger and married her on 17 May 1899 in Mount Airy. His brother, Wilbur Kochtitzky, came to Mount Airy to be the furniture company's bookkeeper in 1901 and married Elizabeth Sparger, Alice's sister, on 31 October 1907. Sometime after, Wilbur opened his own clothing store in Mount Airy and operated it until his death in 1951. (Information from the Kochtitzky Family Association.)

Oscar Wilbur Kochtitzky granite footstone located in Oakdale Cemetery.

Jimmie Trevathan was a fallen officer from Mount Airy. His tombstone, although small and flat, tells a story of a man that gave the ultimate gift of his life for his community through community service and sacrifice. He was shot by a suspect on June 2, 1963 in Mount Airy while trying to apprehend him.

It is foolish and wrong to mourn the men who died, rather We should thank God that such men lived.
- Gen. George S. Patton, Jr.

This Granite Mill Stone has been used as a tombstone for the Badgett Family at the Union Primitive Baptist Church in Surry County, North Carolina. The plaque on the back says that it has been in the Badgett family since 1880 and was placed here in 1976.

The Gianopulos is a Celtic cross carved from Mount Airy Granite. The IHS stands for "in hoc signo vinces," which means "In this sign you will conquer."

Tombstone of J.E. Kirkman, Vice-President of Southern Chair Company.

Located in Oakwood Cemetery in High Point, NC, this tombstone and plot was built with Mount Airy Granite. This plot also belongs to the Kirkman family.

Bowman Gray, Sr. (May 1, 1874-July 7, 1935)

While touring the Salem Cemetery, one cannot miss the obelisk placed in memory of Bowman Gray. It appears to be about 20 feet to 30 feet tall and made from North Carolina Granite. Bowman died while on vacation in Norway and was buried at sea. This memorial provides a spot for his family to remember him. It is surrounded by various members of the Gray family.

Mr. Gray was a former president and chairman of R. J. Reynolds Tobacco Company in Winston-Salem, North Carolina and founder and a major benefactor of Wake Forest University School and Bowman Gray School of Medicine.

Bowman Gray was born in what was then Winston, North Carolina to Wachovia bank co-founder James Alexander Gray and the former Miss Aurelia Bowman. After high school, Gray attended the University of North Carolina at Chapel Hill in the 1890-91 academic years. He left school the following year to become a clerk at Wachovia Bank and Trust Company. In 1895, he began working at R. J. Reynolds Tobacco Company as a salesman. His success in sales propelled him into management after two years, at which point he moved to Baltimore, Maryland, where he married the former Nathalie Fontaine Lyons on October 1, 1902. There their two sons were born, Bowman Gray, Jr. in 1907 and Gordon Gray in 1909.

In 1912, Gray moved his family to Winston-Salem, North Carolina to take up his new position of vice-president and director of R. J. Reynolds Tobacco Company. He was handpicked by Reynolds himself to head the company's finance division. By 1924, he was promoted to president of the company to succeed President William Neal Reynolds. In 1932 he became the chairman of the board of directors. Later, Gray's brother James Gray, Jr. would also become president of R.J. Reynolds.

Between 1927 and 1932, he and his wife oversaw the construction of Graylyn, their 87 acre estate in the countryside surrounding Winston-Salem, located across from R.J. Reynolds' estate, The Reynolda House. They moved into Graylyn in 1932. He and his wife donated their former house for use as a church. It is amazing but during the two years of construction they lived over the garage which is approximately 1500 square feet. Two years after moving to Graylyn, Gray died of a heart attack while vacationing with his family aboard a ship off the coast of Norway. He was buried at sea.

Graylyn was not fully complete until 1952 due to the Great Depression. After Bowman's death, Graylyn was donated to the Bowman School of Medicine, where it served as an academic psychiatric hospital facility until 1959.

At the time of his death in 1935, he left $750,000 worth of stock in R.J. Reynolds Tobacco Company to Wake Forest University for the establishment of a medical school. In 1941, the Bowman Gray School of Medicine opened.

Gray left behind a legacy of giving and philanthropy. The property on which the Centenary Methodist Church sits was donated by Gray. Also, he contributed to other local hospitals and orphanages as well. He and his sons also contributed heavily to Wake Forest University and the University of North Carolina at Chapel Hill. His holdings in R. J. Reynolds alone were valued at $12 million, at the time of his death. At some point, Bowman Gray became a Rotarian like his father, James Alexander Gray, and served the organization well. Records show that Bowman Gray, Jr. was a member by 1937.

Bowman Gray obelisk in the Salem Cemetery.

Albert Einstein Memorial (Washington, DC)

This fabulous monument is located in an Elm and Holly Grove at the National Acadamy of Sciences in Washington, DC. The statue is a bronze sculpture of Albert sitting on Mount Airy Granite. The unveiling happened on April 22, 1979 in honor of his centennial birthday. The statue alone weighs 4 tons. Special supports were used just to hold the statue in place.

Sculpture Robert Berks, famous Kennedy sculptor, designed the statue and landscape architect James A. Van Sweden designed the monument landscaping.

Albert Einstein bronze statue that sits on Mount Airy Granite.

Worth noting are the Einstein quotations engraved in the stone:

1. As long as I have any choice in the matter, I shall live only in a country where civil liberty, tolerance, and equality of all citizens before the law prevail.
2. Joy and amazement of the beauty and grandeur of this world of which man can just form a faint notion.
3. The right to search for truth implies also a duty; one must not conceal any part of what one has recognized to be true.

National World War II Memorial

Built to remember veterans from World War II, this memorial contains 56 pillars and a pair of arches constructed of Mount Airy Granite surrounding a plaza and fountain. It is located on the National Mall where the old Rainbow Reflecting pool is located. Officially, it opened to the public on April 24, 2004. Plans had been made years ago for this memorial. It was dedicated by then President George W. Bush on May 29, 2004. Over 4 million people visit this memorial every year.

A nationwide competition was held for the design of the memorial. Friederich St. Florians submitted the winning design.

Each of the 56 pillars has an engraving to one of the 50 states and District of Columbia, Alaskan Territory, Commonwealth of the Philippines, Puerto Rico, Guam, America Samoa, and the U.S. Virgin Islands. The southern Arch is inscribed Atlantic and the northern arch is inscribed the Pacific.

It is 337 feet 10 inches long and 240 feet 2 inches wide. It is sunk 6 feet below grade and contains a pool that is 246 feet 9 inches by 147 feet 8 inches.

WWII Memorial with the North Carolina Section

Daniel Boone Highway Marker

This Daniel Boone Trail Highway Marker is located in North Wilkesboro, North Carolina. These highway markers were built from parts of the battleship USS Maine and some (like this one) placed on Mount Airy Granite shaped into an arrowhead. There were originally 358 markers from Virginia Beach all the way to San Francisco. Mr. J. Hampton Rich of Mocksville, North Carolina was responsible for this idea to remember Daniel Boone.

Durham Government Complex Monuments

Civil War Monument in Durham

Durham Roll of Honor Monument

Martinsville, Virginia Government Square

On the Courthouse square in Martinsville, Virginia sits this nice granite monument to Brig. General Joseph Martin for whom the city is named.

Fort Fisher Monument

Cemetery Entrance Ways

This is a 1909 blue sky postcard depicting the entrance for the Greenwood Cemetery located in Lancaster, PA, charted on September 4, 1895. It was constructed by D. M. Rothenberger, architect, and Kaufman and Kraemer, contractors and stands in remembrance of them. It was sent from Kathleen to Mrs. John White of Stroudsburg, PA.

The Hurlburt Memorial Gate, Gladin Park, still stands in Detroit, Michigan. This blue sky postcard was postmarked 1912.

CHAPTER 13

Green Hill Cemetery, Greensboro, North Carolina

The entrance to this cemetery is adorned with Mount Airy Granite; a testament to the importance that it played in the early construction of the city. Established in 1895 by the City of Greensboro, this cemetery has a beautiful setting.

Many former city leaders and citizens rest here. Some of the former were crucial in the development of the North Carolina Granite Corporation. They will be discussed along with photos of some of their tombstones and mausoleums.

Half of the entrance way into Green Hill Cemetery built with Mount Airy Granite.

William Martin Roach

Not well known today but definitely well known during the 1920's was a Mr. William Roach. He was born January 13, 1866 in Rockingham County, North Carolina and died July 13, 1927 in Wilimington, New Hanover County, North Carolina from a fall during a construction project. Mr. Roach was a Greensboro business owner of a granite and marble company called Rowe and Roach. Mr. Roach was involved in the construction and supply of many granite buildings and monuments in Greensboro and throughout North Carolina. His company was located on the railroad tracks which made it easier to unload the heavy granite. Also, if he was shipping to another destination it was easier for him to load it from his docks.

Mr. Roach's monument is made of North Carolina Granite and actually looks like a large boulder. It is located in Green Hill Cemetery in Greensboro. His wife, Manie Somers Roach, is buried beside of him. She predeceased him in death. Their only daughter lived in Reidsville, North Carolina.

Mr. Roach died from a fall that he took during construction of the First Presbyterian Church on Third Street in Wilmington, North Carolina. The county coroner's report said that his skull was fractured. The construction of this church was not completed until 1928. Architect Hobert Upjohn was in charge of this project. His plans included architectural styles from three different periods: the Norman, as represented in the Chapel; the English Decorated Gothic (actually Middle Period Gothic with French influence), in the Sanctuary; the Elizabethan, in the Church School Building.

The personal home of Mr. Roach was located across the street from the Greensboro Presbyterian Church on Walker Avenue but has been razed for a parking lot. This location put his home very near the railroad tracks where he would have probably walked to work. It is believed that his home was constructed of Mount Airy Granite.

If anyone left a mark on Greensboro it was William Martin Roach.

The office of Wm. M. Roach formerly located near the Greensboro Depot (above) and his tombstone (below).

William Martin Roach's Mount Airy Granite tombstone and Mount Airy Granite tombstone located in Green Hill Cemetery, Greensboro, NC.

Thomas Woodroffe and Family

Thomas Woodroffe is best known for organizing the Mount Airy Granite Quarry officially on May 14, 1889. For the previous 100 years the quarry had been through many different owners. Since May 14, 1889, the quarry has been in pretty much continuous operation. There are some indications that after Mr. Woodroffe bought the quarry the stone masons across the U.S. went on strike. This delayed many projects including the construction of Ulysses S. Grant's tomb in New York.

Because of the ownership of the quarry, the CF & YVR awarded Mr. Woodroffe the contract to build all of the depots between Mount Airy and Greensboro, North Carolina. Directly after the reconstruction of the United States the CY and YVR was organized from the Mount Airy and the Western Railroad. This line ran from Mount Airy all the way to Wilmington. A very large branch also ran to Bennettsville, South Carolina.

Mr. Woodroffe's family moved from Greensboro to Mount Airy. Their home is still located across from the First Baptist Church of Mount

Airy. It is pink today. When Thomas died in a mining accident at the quarry, his body was taken to Greensboro and buried in the Green Hill Cemetery. As time progressed each of his family members were interred in Green Hill Cemetery or memorialized with a granite marker. Two of the children may have been buried in Texas. These tombstones are small in stature compared to the importance of the family's standing in the community.

The family was known for its beautiful music and architectural projects. On exhibit at the Mount Airy History Museum are numerous items like tea caddy from the 1870s, traveling desk, music books from 1909, an English flute of ivory and wood and an 1892 wedding dress. This is probably from the wedding of one of his children. They were adults by the time he moved to Mount Airy. Many Sunday afternoon concerts were held in the parlor of the Woodroffe home.

Mr. Woodroffe donated the granite for several beautiful buildings located in Mount Airy; the First Baptist Church and Trinity Episcopal, Flat Rock Elementary School, and Flat Rock Baptist Church.

David Schenck Highway Marker

Outside of the cemetery fence sits this historical highway marker dedicated to Judge David Schenck.

Judge David Schenck's monument located at Green Hill Cemetery. He is surrounded by his family and friends. He loved Mount Airy Granite and used it in almost all of the mounuments he placed at Guilford Courthouse Battleground and for his family memorial monuments.

CHAPTER 14

NC STATE BELL TOWER

North Carolina State was organized in 1887 as a land grant university as "The People's University." It was called the North Carolina College of Agriculture and Mechanic Arts. Classes began in the fall of 1889 with a student body of 72 and six faculty members. Today, over 31,000 students call the campus their university. Around 8,000 faculty members call this university their employer. Over 700 buildings exist on the campus as of 2011.

Van Sykes, class of 1907, is credited with the proposal of constructing a memorial bell tower on the campus of North Carolina State as a memorial to the veterans of World War I that were alumni of the university. Architect William Henry Deacy was hired to design and oversee the project in 1920. Jack Sargent was directly involved with supplying granite for the tower.

Memorial Tower honors those alumni who were killed in World War I. The cornerstone was laid in 1921 and the Tower was dedicated on November 11, 1949 by Governor R. Gregg Cherry of Gastonia.

Recognized as the symbol for North Carolina State University, the Memorial Bell Tower is 122   foot tall. It is equipped with carillon bells which ring out the alma mater three times daily. The tower was built with 1400 tons of Mount Airy Granite and stands on 700 tons of concrete. It exceeded the planned cost of $15,000.

Three years after the conclusion of World War I, 1921, the first corner stone was laid, as well as, the first 10 foot section. More sections were added in 1924, 1925, and 1926. Due to the depression, fund raising for the tower slowed after the initial phase. Thus it was not completed until 1937. The WPA (Works Progress Administration) aided in the completion of the tower. The class of 1938 and the honor society, donated the clock and the class of 1939 donated the flood lights.

Although 33 alumni died in WWI, 34 names are listed. Ironically, one of the students was thought to have expired in the war, G. L. Jeffers, class of 1913, was found alive and well back in the States. The error was not corrected before the plate was made so it was altered to G.E. Jefferson to all unknown veterans of State lost in war.

After WWII the finishing details were completed (chimes, shrine room, and memorial plaque). On November 11, 1949, it was dedicated by Governor R. Gregg Cherry. In March of 1986, the new carillon in the tower was dedicated to honor Dr. Carey Bostian, former chancellor and his wife, Neita.

In the summer of 2008, work began to remodel the tower due to affects of the weather. Water was draining in the windows and draining down into the tower and destroying the mortar. Severe freezing and thawing were also damaging the interior of the shrine room. Many years of weather had discolored the stone. The solution was to wash the outside of the tower and redo the mortar joints.

The marble in the shrine room was dismantled and a waterproof enclosure built then the marble was reinstalled.

The cobblestone walkway was dismantled and completely redone.

In 2009, the tower sustained damage from a lightning strike. A capstone was knocked out of place. Although built with Mount Airy Granite, the tower requires constant maintenance and this year, 2011, construction began to reseal the mortar joints up to the first 18 feet.

Special Lighting Events of the Bell Tower

On special holidays the bell tower is lighted with red bulbs. Some of these include Memorial Day and Veterans Day.

Other events celebrated by the campus community when the tower is lighted include:

- Commencements: Spring and Winter
- On Founders Day, NC State Remembers – the annual day of remembrance honoring our Founders and members of our NC State University who have passed away.
- At the induction of a member of the NC State Faculty into the National Academy of Sciences or National Academy of Engineering
- The awarding of a Nobel Prize, Pulitzer Prize, National Medal of Science, or National Medal of Technology.
- Awards: North Carolina Award or Governor's Award for Excellence, O Max Gardner Award, the Board of Governors' Award for Excellence in Teaching, Public Service.

- The selection of scholarships: Clarendon Oxford, Gates Cambridge, Goldwater, Madison, Marshall, Mitchell, Rhodes, Truman, or Udall.
- For the inauguration of the President of the University of North Carolina or installation of the Chancellor of NC State.
- Sports Victories, home and away for football, basketball, men's and women's, ACC Championship victories, and
- Other celebrations at the discretion of the Chancellor.

NC State Bell Tower

Close up of the clock and the carved eagles on the NC State Bell Tower.

NC State DAR Monument

DAR Monument to the 13 Colonies built of Mount Airy Granite located on the NC State Campus.

CHAPTER 15

GUILFORD COURTHOUSE BATTLEGROUND

So what does the Guilford Courthouse Battleground have to do with Mount Airy Granite? Well, bear with me and I'll tell you about their connection.

The Revolutionary War played out in our back door with a pivotal battle occurring in Guilford County between General Nathanael Greene, commander of the American forces, and Lord Charles Cornwallis, commander of the British Forces. Because of the success of the regulators in this battle, America won the war as it concluded in Yorktown, Virginia. This battle occurred on a wet March 15, 1781. By far, it was the most contested battle up to that day during the war. General Greene defended the property with 4,500 American militiamen. Twenty-five percent of his men lost their lives on this day. Although not a great victory for Greene, this particular battle caused Lord Cornwallis to abandon his efforts at occupying the Carolinas and he focused on Yorktown, Virginia.

General Greene was born to Quaker parents in 1742 in Rhode Island. It is no coincidence that this major battle took place near the Quaker settlement of New Garden. Appointed early in the war by George Washington, he had been reluctant to take charge. During the three previous years he had proven himself as a very capable leader in the southern campaign. Due to his wit and cunning, the British troops were worn down.

During the war, he gave his personal word to contractors that they would be paid for supplies. To stand by his word, he sold almost all of his worldly possessions to pay the debt after the war.

Greensborough, now Greensboro, North Carolina is named for this patriotic American who fought the British for freedom.

We come to the late 1800's and early 1900's to find our connection to Mount Airy Granite Company. All of the monuments in this park are crafted from Mount Airy Granite. Twenty-eight graves and monuments are located within the park and the headstones are also of granite.

Judge David Schenck (1835-1902) saved the Guilford Courthouse Battleground. Schenck, a lawyer by profession, moved to Guilford County from Lincolnton County, North Carolina after retiring in the early 1881. Upon his arrival he accepted a position of general counsel to the

Richmond and Danville Railroad. Many afternoons he would take his horse and buggy and drive to the battleground, make notes, and study previous diaries about the battle. On one such visit he decided to buy up the land and develop the Guilford Battleground Company. Once purchased, he cleaned up the property. He purchased 42 acres of the battleground property almost 100 years after the battle. Unfortunately, it had become cluttered with underbrush, trees, and shrubs of the wild nature. He transferred it to the Guilford Battleground Co. on May 6, 1887.

Judge David Schenck in his youth.

He is buried at Green Hill Cemetery (See the chapter 13 on Green Hill Cemetery). A historical highway marker on Guilford Battleground next to the cemetery tells his story.

The first monument was placed in 1887 and was cut from Mount Airy Granite. Over the next several years over 32 monuments were erected.

Two granite arches were erected on July 4, 1906. They were 12 feet wide by 20 feet high. The granite archways were removed because no cars could go through them. The Davidson Memorial Arch was removed and rebuilt at Davidson College near Mooresville, North Carolina.

Standing in the Guilford Courthouse National Park is a very large statue of General Greene on his mount. The base of the statue is carved from North Carolina Granite. In 1911, the U.S. Government appropriated $30,000 for the construction of the monument. It was erected on July 3, 1915 by the Guilford Battleground Company after a grant from the federal government for $30,000. It was sculpted by Frances H. Packer.

The Mrs. Kerren-Happuch Turner is for the memory of this very brave woman. She had seven sons that served in the Revolutionary War along with her grandsons that fought for General Greene. During the battle she nursed the wounded soldiers at the battle of Guilford Courthouse. This is first monument on a battlefield for a woman. The Guilford Courthouse Battleground was the first Revolutionary Battlefield bought and restored for the Revolutionary War.

MONUMENT TO THE MARYLAND LINE ON GUILFORD BATTLE-FIELD,
DEDICATED 15 OCTOBER, 1892.

This is a vintage photo of the Nathaniel Greene Monument taken sometime after the turn of the century.

Current view of the Nathaniel Greene Monument

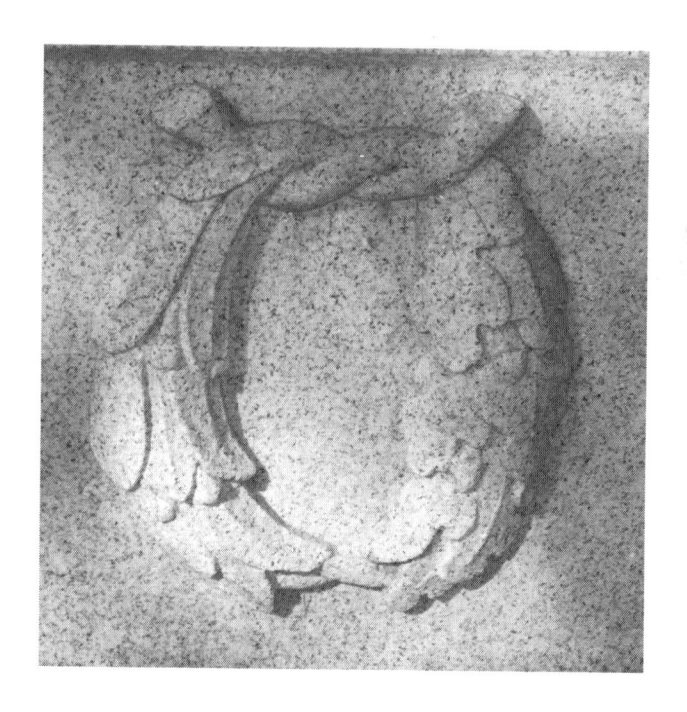

Carved wreath located on the side of the Nathaniel Greene Monument at Guilford Battleground.

215

Colonial Monument (James Hunter/Alamance Battleground)

This blue sky postcard is of the Colonial Monument located at the Guilford Battle Ground. The base of the statue is Mount Airy Granite.

    This monument was dedicated in 1901 and then transferred to the Alamance Battleground in 1962. The National Park Service believed it better served the public at the Alamance Battlegroud and they are correct. You can see it today in all of its glory in the middle of the battleground.

Joseph Winston Monument

Unveiled in 1895, this monument to Joseph Winston was sponsored by then Gov. Hunt.

Winston and Franklin

The graves of Joseph Winston, Major of Surry County Militia, and Jessee Franklin, Maj. Of Continental Line and Governor of North Carolina. Tombstones are made with Mount Airy Granite with a metal plate attached.

Governor Franklin's remains were removed from Low Gap, Surry County, North Carolina and interred here sometime after the park was formed. He also served as senator for North Carolina from 1799 to 1805 and also from 1807 to 1813. He served as President Pro Tempore of the Senate in the Eighth Congress. He was appointed a Commissioner to treat with the Chickasaw Indians in 1817, and was elected Governor of North Carolina, serving from 1820 to 1821.

Major Joseph Winston is the name sake for Winston-Salem. Originally he was interred in Stokes County but reinterred to the about the same time as Major/Governor Franklin. He served at the battle of Kings Mountain.

Peter Francisco (Calvary) Monument

The plaque on the Granite Obelisk reads: "To Peter Francisco, A Giant in Stature, Might and Courage, who slew in his engagement eleven of the enemy with his broad sword rendering himself thereby perhaps the most famous private soldier of the Revolutionary War."

Schenck

Plaque reads: David Schenck, The Projector of this Battlefield Reclamation and Organization and First President of the Guilford Battleground Company, 1835-1902.

Reynolds and Stevens

Granite Monuments to Captain George Reynolds and Brig. Gen. Edward Stevens who was wounded while making his gallant stand with the Virginia Troops.

Hooper-Penn-Hewes Monument

William Hooper, signer of the Declaration of Independence, monument.
One of the most impressive monuments at the park.

Plaque on the William Hooper monument

Three of the signers of the Declaration of Independence are interred at Guilford Courthouse Battleground and they are William Hooper of Hillsborough, Joseph Hewes of Edenton, and John Penn of Williamsboro, Granville County.

William Hooper, born in Boston, Massachusetts, on June 17, 1742, and died on October 14, 1790, was originally buried in Hillsboro but his body was reinterred to Greensboro in the late 1800s. He was a lawyer, Supreme Court Justice, North Carolina Attorney General, and delegate to the Continental Congress.

Joseph Hewes was born in Kingston, New Jersey on January 23, 1730 and died on November 10, 1779. He was educated at what is now Princeton University. He moved to Wilmington and began a prosperous mercantile and shipping business. He served in the Provincial Assembly State House of Commons and as a member of the Continental Congress.

John Penn was born May 17, 1741 in Caroline County, Virginia and died September 14, 1788 near Williamsboro. He was also a lawyer, member of the Continental Congress, and a North Carolina representative.

Mrs. Keren Happuch Turner Monument

This is the first monument dedicated to a woman to be placed on an American battlefield. It was manufactured by M.H. Mullins of Salem, Ohio and J. Segesman was the Sculptor. Plaque reads: "A heroine of '75, Mrs. Keren Happuch Turner, mother of Elizabeth, the wife of Joseph Morehead of N.C. and grandmother of Captain James and of John Morehead, a young soldier under Greene who rode horse-back from her Maryland home and at Guilford Court House Nursed to health a badly wounded son."

The Gillies Monument

"GILLIES"
"Light Horse Harry Lee's Bugler-Boy"
This monument was erected by the Oak Ridge Military Academy to the memory of the Gallant Gillies who fell under the swords of Tarleton's Dragoons on Feb. 12th, 1781, a noble generosity that sacrificed his own for his country's freedom. Erected on May 6th, 1898.

Above: An educational plaque about Monument Row

Below: Grave of Major John Daves (his body was reinterred here in June 1893). He was the grandfather of the first NC State Regent of the DAR.

No North-No South Monument

Erected in 1903 and commemorates the year 1776 and General Greene.

The park founders had no intention of recreating the battlefield but to provoke thought in the public and appreciation for the men that fought and died here. They created "pleasuring" grounds that are quite peaceful. Thirty two monuments turned the battleground into a landscape of ideas, spotlighting certain aspects of the battle.

In 1937, the National Park Service took over the Guilford Courthouse Battleground and renamed it the Guilford Courthouse Military Park. With the new administration they decided to focus on the Revolutionary War battle that took place here. Using the WPA work force, they removed several monuments that had nothing to do with the battle including this beautiful Davidson Arch. Courtesy of the NPS.

Walking around the park you can find left over granite.

CHAPTER 16

KRESS DEPARTMENT STORES

Samuel Henry Kress (1863-1955) opened his first dime store in 1896 in Memphis, Tennessee. They were called "S. H. Kress & Company." He was from Cherryville, Pennsylvania. By 1944 over 200 stores were open. The most distinctive stores were designed by Edward F. Sibbert (1899-1982). They were built from the beginning of the depression through World War II.

Although America was in a deep depression, Kress realized that it would not last forever and took advantage of the cheap labor and materials to build his unique art deco designs. The façade of the Greensboro store still has the beautiful color tiles inserted. He used the highest standard of materials and employed around 100 people in the design department. While varied on the outside, the inside had a standard for displays and organization.

This art deco is still on the former Kress Department Store building in Greensboro, NC. The flowers are actually in a variety of colors.

Kress was a lover of art, especially that of the Italian Renaissance. This is clearly shown in the design of the store fronts which were carved from Mount Airy Granite. At the age of 65, he established the Kress Foundation to promote understanding and appreciation of European art in the United States. Kress was a major early donor to the U.S. National Gallery of Art.

After World War 11, Kress extended its retail operations into the suburbs. Genesco, Inc. took over Kress in 1964 and began closing unprofitable stores and then liquidated the company in 1980. As main street preservation programs took hold, Kress buildings, along with other older structures that were subject to demolition. Determined activists recognized the value of protecting early commercial architecture. Thus many of the stores have been reused as offices, restaurants, and retail shops, furthering the purposes of downtown revitalization. Because of these efforts, the architectural heritage of S. H. Kress & Co. can still be seen today on main streets across America. The Greensboro Kress building is hosts a night club and coffee shop.

Now put to other uses, a number of former Kress stores, are ranked as landmarks. Some of the most well-known Kress locations included New York City's Fifth Avenue, Canal Street, New Orleans, and one at Hollywood's Sunset Boulevard. The one at Sunset Boulevard is now preserved as a theme park in Florida.

In 1980, Kress went out of business and was purchased by McCrory Stores Corporation, which filed for bankruptcy in 1992. Kress department stores operated from 1896 until 1981.

Kress Department Store

Here is a vintage postcard of the Main Kress Department Store in New York.

Kress in Durham (Art Deco)

The Kress Building located in Durham, North Carolina. This one is art deco with very little granite used in the facing of the building.

CHAPTER 17

Granite Courthouses

Alamance County Courthouse (1923, Graham, North Carolina)
    The current courthouse opened to the public on November 23, 1924 at a cost of $253,925.82. The courthouse was built in the Classical Revival style and features Mount Airy Granite, terracotta stonework, dentil moulding, and metal- masonry floors. Originally, the courthouse housed the court system, county government offices, the sheriff's office, state government offices, agricultural offices, health department offices, and federal offices. The sheriff's original office is located in the southwestern 1st floor corner of the building. It features metal-framed shatter-resistant windows. The 2nd floor courtroom ceiling is silk. In 1979, the Courthouse was added to the National Register of Historic Places. It sits in the middle of a traffic circle.

Alamance County, North Carolina Courthouse

Guilford County Courthouse (1918, Greensboro, North Carolina)

Designed by Architect Harry Barton of Greensboro, the Guilford County Courthouse was constructed with Mount Airy Granite. During the construction period, a granite yard was established next to the building. That is to be expected with the size of the building. Considering the many projects being constructed by Harry Barton's firm they would need a large quantity of granite in and around town.

The building is still in use today, but not for court. It has a lovely tiled floor dating from the construction period. Large wooden doors greet the visitor upon entering the building. For convenience and the handicapped, a small elevator was added later.

Guilford County Courthouse

This building shows a wonderful example of stone masonry. Carved into the upper side of the building is "Guilford County Courthouse." All of this carving would have been done by hand with the precision of a laser.

Surry County Courthouse (1916, Dobson, North Carolina)

The third courthouse for Surry County was built in 1916 and designed by Harry Barton. He offered two exterior choices for the Courthouse. The first design was presented to be built with Mount Airy Granite. The second one, which was chosen, only used a small percentage of granite. It was built with bricks being made from the local Dobson Clay. This clay gives it a peach hue. The trim is Mount Airy granite. Economic recession hit the county hard and thus prevented a granite courthouse from being constructed. Half-way through the project the county leaders chose the Dobson brick option.

The original drawings were discovered in 2010 in a room in the old courthouse. Current Register of Deeds, Carolyn Comer, had the drawings perseved for future generations to view in an acid free environment. They are located in the register of deeds office in a red binder.

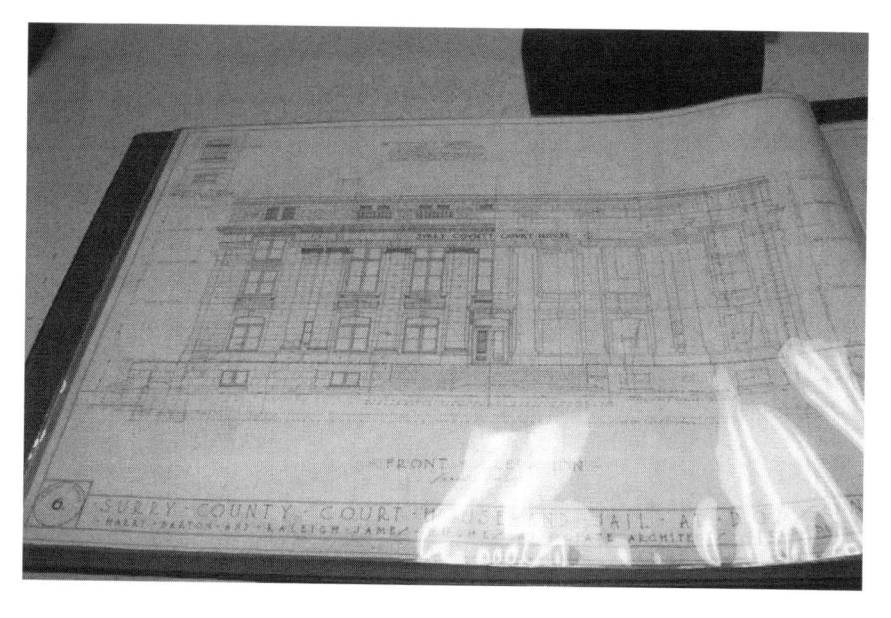

The drawings were hand drawn exquisitely by Mr. Barton and his partner, James Hughes of Greensboro, NC. These drawings show that one extra floor was offered as an option called the penthouse for the jailer. The jail was to be located on the top floor. Rooms to be located on this floor included a kitchen, store room, one juvenile cell with bunk beds, toilet, and sink, cells for white women with bunk beds, toilet, and sink, rooms for colored women with bunk beds, toilet, and sink, rooms for white men with bunk beds, toilet, and sink, and rooms for black men with toilet, and sink. Also offered on the jail floor was an insane ward that contained a portable padded cell. The shower is located in the hallway with no privacy. All of the windows on this floor were to have metal grills.

Early court days at the Surry County Courthouse in Dobson, NC

Civil War Marker located in Dobson at the Surry County Courthouse and built with Mount Airy Granite.

The second Surry County Courthouse designed by Harry Barton.

Cornerstone marker noting the general contractor that completed the upgrades to the Harry Barton and James Hughes design of the Surry County Courthouse.

Alleghany County, Virginia Courthouse

Alleghany County Courthouse, Covington, Virginia

New Hanover County, North Carolina Courthouse

New Hanover Courthouse, Wilmington, North Carolina has granite surrounding the entrance ways, windows, and details. Now used as a visitors center.

Archway close up of the New Hanover County Courthouse in Wilmington, North Carolina.

Randolph County Courthouse

Randolph County Courthouse and the Civil War Monument both have a base of Mount Airy Granite. (Vintage Postcard)

Asheboro is the county seat for Randolph County, North Carolina. The geographical center of North Carolina is just south of Asheboro in Seagrove, the pottery capital of the World.

Henry County Courthouse

This vintage photo of the Henry County Courthouse is built with brick but all of the steps, retaining walls, and base of the monuments are Mount Airy Granite.

The Henry County Courthouse is located in Martinsville, Virginia, an independent city. This is a southwestern county of Virginia. Martinsville was founded by an American Revolutionary War General, Joseph Martin. He was good friends with Patrick Henry for whom Henry County is named.

For many years, Henry County was known as the "Plug Chewing Tobacco Capital" of the world. The furniture industry took the place of the tobacco industry in the early 1900s. Textiles became the next economic staple.

Old Guilford Courthouse Sign

This Mount Airy Granite sign documented the origional Guilford Courthouse which was located in the center of Guilford County in the late 1700's. Although, the courthouse itself was not granite but log. The founders of the Guilford Courthouse Battleground Company wanted a lasting rememberance as a memorial to the ment that fought here on March 15, 1781.

CHAPTER 18

Mount Airy Granite Overlook on the Blue Ridge Parkway

The Blue Ridge Parkway celebrated its 75th Anniversary on September 11, 2010. Construction began on September 11, 1935 near the North Carolina State Line and the Virginia State Line at Cumberland Knob. It is a 469 mile highway that rest along the ridges of the Blue Ridge Mountains. It starts in Waynesboro, Virginia and ends in Cherokee, North Carolina covering 19 counties.

The parkway was part of President Franklin D. Roosevelt's New Deal. During the Depression of the 1930s many Americans were out of work. The New Deal provided jobs through the Civilian Conservation Corps (CCC) Camps, the Works Project Administration (WPA), and various other programs. Men across the country joined these programs and were stationed near their jobs.

On the Blue Ridge Parkway, four CCC camps were built. They were managed military style with a strict schedule. First the camps were established as a tent town. Once the men arrived they built the necessary buildings. The four camps were Camp Kelso near Bedford, Virginia, Rocky Knob Camp, near Meadows of Dan, Virginia, Doughton Park, near Sparta, North Carolina, and one near Black Mountain, North Carolina.

The first section of the parkway was 12.965 miles. Work did not follow a linear path but rather was bid out in sections. Companies from across the nation bid for the road work.

The CCC boys did the landscaping, built buildings, picnic tables, and much of the hands on projects. The companies were hired with heavy equipment to actually build the road. In North Carolina Nelo Teer received the first awarded bid and in Virginia, Albert Brothers Contractors from Salem, Virginia received the second awarded bid.

Heavy equipment was hauled by train to Galax, Virginia. Then it was either driven or hauled to Cumberland Knob.

Stanley W. Abbott was the first landscape architect hired by the park service to design the parkway. He surveyed the land from Waynesboro, Virginia to Cherokee, North Carolina by foot. The states involved had a great debate over the chosen path. Robert Doughton from Sparta pushed for the parkway to go through Alleghany County instead of Tennessee. He won.

Stanley W. Abbott designed the buildings, the fences, the signs, and the whole atmosphere of the parkway. Born in Yonkers, New York, he was educated at Cornell University. His career started at Finger Lakes State Park.

Mr. Abbott set strict standards for each item on the parkway; one of those being the blue gray paint that is still used today. It blends in to the country as do the style of the buildings. Another strict guideline that he established was that the bridges, culverts, and over passes were to be faced with stone, local stone. In the beginning proposals were made by various companies to provide stone. Mount Airy Granite put in a proposal to provide granite for the structures. Eventually they were turned down due to the fact that they were over 15 miles from the parkway and the guideline required the stone to be within 15 miles of the parkway. The shipping costs would have been too much for the parkway budget.

With the parkway having many overlooks built to view the beautiful surrounding hills and valleys, one of the overlooks built was the Mount Airy Granite Overlook. The educational sign describes the white spot off in the distance as the Quarry.

Today, the surrounding trees have grown so tall that you cannot see the quarry from the overlook but someone has placed a large piece of granite near the educational sign so that the viewer can see what it looks like.

Mount Airy Granite overlook located on the Blue Ridge Parkway, Fancy Gap, Virginia

CHAPTER 19

MORE GRANITE BUILDINGS

Jefferson Standard Insurance Building
(101 North Elm Street, Greensboro, NC)

Standing 233 feet tall, the Jefferson Standard Insurance building was completed in 1923. The original section of the building has 18 floors. Jefferson Standard Life Insurance was founded August 7, 1907 in Raleigh, NC. It was patriotically named for Thomas Jefferson.

Eager to expand, the company absorbed Security Life and Annuity Company and Greensboro Life Insurance Company, subsequently transferring its headquarters to Greensboro. The year 1912 also marked the beginning of an era of expanding prosperity for Jefferson Standard Insurance. Under the direction of Julian Price they grew by leaps and bounds. He was noted as an articulate man of vision and combined skills of sales, a deep sense of ethics, and top notch skills in finance.

Under Price, he was deeply devoted to building in the South and provided much needed finances to farmers and industrialist. Many of the homes in Greensboro were financed through his company.

Julian Price was born on November 25, 1867 in Richmond, Virginia. He was the son of Joseph Jones Price and Margaret Hill Price. He married Ethel Clay and they had two children, Kathleen Marshall Price that married Joseph McKinley Bryan and Ralph Clay Price. Julian Price died on October 25, 1946 in North Wilkesboro in an automobile accident. His body is interred a the Green Hill Cemetery in Greensboro. He was probably coming home from an outing at his land in the mountains. His son took over with Jefferson Standard Life Insurance Company for the next four years as its president.

Today a very large campground on the Blue Ridge Parkway is called the Julian Price Park. This land was Julian Price's private oasis of 3,500 acres directly adjacent to the Moses Cone Manor. This land is now the largest developed land on the parkway for public use. The man made lake is called Price Lake in his honor.

JEFFERSON STANDARD LIFE INSURANCE COMPANY'S BUILDING.

A vintage linen postcard with some of the first Model A's shows the importance of the Jefferson Pilot Standard Life Insurance Company to the economy of Greensboro. This building was listed on the National Register of Historic Places on May 28, 1976.

    Julian Price was a member of the Rotary Club of Greensboro and several other civic organizations.
    The company now is known as the Lincoln Financial Group. Until the Nissen building was completed in 1927 in Winston-Salem, it was the tallest building in North Carolina.
    The president of the company was Julian C. Price of Greensboro.

He believed in paying cash for everything and having zero debt. He paid for the building in full before it was built. New York Architect, Charles C. Hartmann, was hired to design the "U" shaped building. The exterior is granite and terra cotta. A bust of Thomas Jefferson is above the door.

In 1967 the company merged with the Pilot Life Insurance and the name was changed to the Jefferson Pilot Life Insurance Corporation. Their headquarters was based in Greensboro until 2006 when it moved to Pennsylvania.

This building was added to the National Registry of Historic Places on May 28, 1976.

BB & T Bank (Mount Airy, North Carolina)

Branch Banking and Trust (BB & T) building located on Main Street in Mount Airy was constructed of polished granite.

BB & T is a North Carolina bank that dates its history back to 1887 in Wilson County when a Civil War Veteran, Alpheus Branch, bought out Thomas Jefferson Hadley's bank. As private bankers, Branch and Hadley accepted time deposits, paid interest and loaned money to help rebuild the farms and small businesses in the community. Area farmers planted their fields in cotton in the early 1880s and with a place to borrow money at reasonable interest; they experimented with a new money crop, tobacco. The company morphed into the business that we see today throughout the south.

RBC Bank, Mount Airy, North Carolina

RBC Bank is unique because small squares of granite were used to construct this building. The former S. M. Hale site.

Formerly Centura Bank, the Royal Bank of Canada (RBC) Bank has a prosperous history also. On November 2, 1990, Centura Bank and Peoples Bankcorp and Planters Corporation of Rocky Mount, North Carolina merged.

In June of 2001, the Royal Bank of Canada bought Centura Banks and renamed it RBC Centura and then in April of 2008, it was renamed RBC Bank.

On June 9, 2011, RBC was purchased by PNC Financial Services.

Municipal Building of Mount Airy, North Carolina

U.S. Department of Agriculture (Washington, DC)

Built in the early 1900's, the U.S. Department of Agriculture building is still in use today and is located directly across from the Holocaust Museum in Washington, D.C.

Immanuel Lutheran College, Greensboro, NC

This beautiful building was razed many years ago. It once stood where the North Carolina A & T Campus stands now at the intersection of Benbow Road and East Market Street. This college was founded in 1903 and moved to Greensboro in 1905 from Concord, North Carolina, for the purpose of preparing African American students for work in theology and education in North Carolina. The campus was composed of 13 acres and the building was completed in 1907. The college was very successful and graduated many students. By 1927 sixteen of the board members on the Church's mission board were graduates of Immanuel.

By 1955, Immanuel had an annual enrollment of 100 students with 10 faculty members. It was supported by the Lutheran Church and owned by the Synodical Conference of North Carolina. Even though it was very successful the Lutheran church chose to close the school in 1961, disposing of the property and buildings rather quickly. They sold the land and buildings to North Carolina A& T University in 1965.

No longer standing, this was the predecessor to the NC A & T University. Vintage Curt Teich & Company linen postcard of the Immanuel Luthern College, main building, Greensboro, North Carolina. This postcard is circa 1907–1910.

Union Trust Building (American Bar Association in Washington, DC)

Designed by Waddy Butler Wood and his firm, Wood, Donn, and Deming, this bank became the first high rise bank to be designed by local architects in the DC area. It was completed in 1906. It is built with red brick and detailed with Mount Airy Granite.

North Carolina Capitol Grounds

On May 27, 1895, the Civil War Soldier Statue at the North Carolina Capitol Grounds was unveiled. Leopold Von Miller, II, was the sculptor and Muldoon Monument Company built the monument. It stands 75 feet tall and cost $22,000 in 1895. It was unveiled by Julian Jackson Christian, Granddaughter of General Stonewall Jackson.

United States Bullion

The U.S. Bullion stores the gold reserves for the United States. It is a fortified vault located adjacent to Fort Knox. Contained in the vault are 4,578 metric tons (5046 tons) of gold bullion (147.2 million oz. troy). Roughly, this is 2.5% of all the gold ever refined throughout human history.

It was built in the early 1930's and the first gold shipment made to the vault was in 1937.

This is a vintage linen postcard of the U.S. Bullion in Kentucky which is built with Mount Airy Granite.

The Wanamaker Store, Philadelphia, PA

The Wanamaker Department Store occupied a whole city block in Philadelpia at the turn of the century. The building was twelve stories high, three stories below the street level and contained 45 acres of floor space. It was the first department store in Philadelphia. There was also one in New York in the early 20th century. At the end of the century there were 16 Wanamaker outlets and they were absorbed by Hect's and eventually Macy's.

The founder of Wanamaker's was John Wanamaker. Unable to serve in the Civil war because of his health, he and his brother-in-law started a men's clothing store in Philadelphia. After the former owner's death, Mr. Wanamaker purchased the old railroad depot to have a larger retail facility. He was a practicing Christian and refused to advertise on Sunday. In 1876 at the centennial celebration of the United States, the Wanamaker Store was a big hit.

Former Greensboro Bank and Trust

The Greensboro Bank and Trust Company building today. The first level is constructed with Mount Airy Granite, as well as the top.

Post Offices

The Dobson Post Office

Vintage Postcard of the Siler City Post Office

CHAPTER 20

FDR FOUR FREEDOMS PARK

The Four Freedoms Park was established to honor the late President Franklin D. Roosevelt. He made is his Four Freedoms Speech in 1941. The island was renamed in Roosevelt's honor in 1973. The Franklin and Eleanor Roosevelt Institute razed funds for the memorial park to keep it going over time. During the 1960's, New York City Mayor, John Lindsay, proposed to reinvent the island. The old hospital was in ruins and the island needed a fresh start. Governor Nelson Rockefeller and Mayor Lindsay announced the plans in 1973.

In 1972, Louis Kahn, one of America's most renowned architects of the 20th century, was asked to design the park; unfortunately this turned out to be only two years before his death. He was carrying the designs with him when he died in Penn Station, New York. When he died, Mitchell and Giurgola Architects kept to Kahn's original intentions with the plans. Vicissitudes and the New York economy delayed monetary gains needed to construct the memorial. Renewed interest arose in 2005 when an exhibit was held in Kahn's memory. Ground breaking took place in 2010 with the completion expected in 2012. Once the park is open it will become a New York State Park.

What are the four freedoms that FDR spoke about? They are the basic freedoms of Americans, the freedom of speech and expression, the freedom of worship, freedom from want, and the freedom from fear. The last two he inserted and are not in the Constitution.

Roosevelt Island, also known as Welfare Island from 1921 through 1973, and before that as Blackwell's Island, sits in the middle of the East River in New York City, between the islands of Manhattan and Queens. Roosevelt Island is approximately 2 miles long and 800 feet wide and a total area of 147 acres.

Roosevelt Island, triangular shaped, is owned by the city of New York for 99 years beginning in 1969. In 1976 a new tramway was added to and from the island for transportation. In 2010 it was updated and modernized. The island is also accessible by bus and subway. It was designed to be car free from the beginning but a limited number of cars are there each day.

The island is supported by a post office, library, a vacuum waste system, and the New York City School System.

Former President Franklin D. Roosevelt in the office and making the Four Freedoms Speech delivered on January 6, 1941.

Here are several slabs of granite that will be heading to the FDR Four Freedom Parks in New York. Courtesy of Mondee Tilley with the Mount Airy News.

FDR Four Freedoms Room during construction. Courtesy of Amiaga Photographers, Inc.

The Northwest Elevation Room during construction. Courtesy of Brennan Photogrpahy

FDR bust inspection upon delivery.

Aerial View of Roosevelt Island – Photo courtesy of Amiaga Photographers, Inc.

Promenade and Monumental Stair – Digital Rendering Courtesy of Christopher Shelley

FDR Four Freedoms Room, Interior Construction View. Digital Rendering Courtesy of Brennan Photography

FDR Four Freedoms Room from the East River will contain carvings listing the four freedoms. Digital Rendering Courtesy of Christopher Shelley

FDR Sculpture Court containing a sculpture of Roosevelt by Jo Davidson. Digital Rendering Courtesy of Christopher Shelley

Good Solid Granite Humor

Q: What kind of music do rocks like? A: Hard Rock

Q: What did the boy volcano say to the girl volcano? A: I lava you!

Q: What is the difference between a geologist and a chemist?
A: A chemist will drink anything that is distilled.
A: A geologist will drink anything that is fermented.

Watson: Holmes! What kind of rock is this? Holmes: Sedimentary, my dear Watson.

Q: What do you do with a dead geologist? A: You Barium them!

One Liners:
Did you hear oxygen and magnesium got together? OMg!
My Sediments exactly!
Geologists are down to "earth" people Geology Rocks, I really dig it.
Have a gneiss day.
 My rocks are gneiss, don't take them for granite.
 May the Quartz be with you!
Geologists probe crevices.
Kiss a geologist and feel the earthquake.
Geologists have their faults.
It's a hard rock life, Rock On!
Geologists can be very sedimental.
I may have many faults, but they are all normal.

source:
http://www.jokes4us.com/miscellaneousjokes/schooljokes/geologyjokes.html

North Carolina Granite Corporation Timeline

Early 1800's possibly used by the Moravians.
1872 – John Gilmer sold "The Rock" for almost nothing to Thomas Woodroffe & Sons of Greensboro, North Carolina.
1889 – Woodroffe built railroad spur of the Cape Fear & Yadkin Railroad between Mount Airy and Greensboro. He received a contract with the railroad to build the depots between Mount Airy and Greensboro. The Mount Airy Depot built with granite.
1910 – John D. "Jack" Sargent hired by Woodroffe as superintendent of the quarry.
1918 – J. D. Sargent Granite Company was organized.
1920's – Christopher Binder, born in Maine, is the General Manager.
 Robert Browne was the superintendent of finishing.
 William S. Martin was Secretary and Treasure.
 Raymond Sargent was the Superintendent of the quarry.
The Quarry was owned by 4 men:
John D. "Jack" Sargent, President
Col. Francis "Frank" Henry Fries – Banker
William F. Shaffner – Banker
Charles B. Keesee – Banker
???? – J. P. Frank hired by Jack Sargent.
???? - J. P. Frank became President of NCGC. He was President for 45 years.
1970 – Mr Frank, President
 Mr. Frank Smith, Vice President and Secretary
 R. Morgan Simmons, Chairman of the Board
1991 – Lacy S. Vernon, President & CEO
1992 – A new building was constructed.
 Lacy Vernon, President.
1993 – Donald R. Shelton, President and CEO
From 1993 to 2001 the same.
2002 – Robert Ferris, President and CEO
From 2002 – 2007 same.
2007 – William Swift, President and CEO

Vintage linen postcard of the Pennsylvania Monument located in Salisbury, North Carolina at the National Cemetery

Bibliography

Books

Black, Allison Harris; An Architectural History of Burlington, NC; Sponsored by the Historic Commission of the City of Burlington, © 1987.

Brown, Marvin A., Greensboro, An Architectural History; © 1995
Dietrich, Richard V., *Petrology of Moutn Airy "Granite; Vol. LIV, No. 6"*; Virginia Polytechnical Insitute © April 1961.

Cameron, Bud; Research on the Scottish Stonecutters

Hampton, Vernon B., History of the Martinsville Rotary Club; © 1965.
Keesee, Vincent A., The Keesee Family in Pittsylvania County, Virginia; © 2000.

Little-Stokes, Ruth, An Inventory of Historic Greensboro: Greensboro, North Carolina; © 1976.

Phillips, Laura A. W.; Simple Treasures: The Architectural Legacy of Surry County; Winston Printing Company, Winston-Salem, North Carolina, © 1987 by the Surry County Historical Society.

Tursi, Frank, Winston-Salem, A History; Blair Publishing, Winston-Salem, North Carolina, © 1994

Unknown Author, A Memorial Volume of the Guilford Battle Ground, Guilford Battleground Company, published by Reece & Elam, Power Job Printers, Greensboro, North Carolina, © 1893.

Young, Douglas M., Morobullia: Seventy Five Years of Winston-Salem Rotary; Winston- Salem Rotary Club © 1992.

Web Pages

American Mausoleum's http://www.americanmausoleums.com/

Barton, Harry (1876-1937) : NC Architects & Builders : NCSU ncarchitects.lib.ncsu.edu/people/P000057

Friends of Green Hill Cemetery http://www.friendsofGreen Hillcemetery.org/

History of the Iroquois Indians
http://www.accessgenealogy.com/native/tribes/iroquioi/iroquoishist.htm

FDR Four Freedoms Park http://www.fdrfourfreedomspark.org/home

First Flight Society http://www.firstflight.org/news.php

New River Notes http://www.newrivernotes.com/va/nuckolls1.htm

First Presbyterian Church of Wilmington
http://www.firstonthird.org/AboutUs/OurHistory/tabid/259/Default.aspx

Guilford Courthouse National Military Park
http://guilfordcourthouse.info/monuments/default.htm

Guilford Battleground Company http://guilfordbattlegroundcompany.org/about/history/

Main Street Five- and-Dime: The Architectural Heritage of S. H. Kress & Co.http://www.nbm.org/Exhibits/past/2000_1996/Main_Street.html:

Makers of America: Biographies http://www.ebooksread.com/authors   eng/

National Park Service for the Wright Brothers
http://www.nps.gov/wrbr/historyculture/thefirstflight.htm

North Carolina Granite Corporation http://www.ncgranite.com/

North Carolina State Archives Library Blog
http://www.lib.unc.edu/blogs/ncm/index.php/2007/06/page/2/

Remembering the House of Kress
http://www.epcc.edu/nwlibrary/sites/ep/kress/narrative.html

Surry County Historical Society of North Carolina http://surrycounty.pastperfect-online.com/

Tannenbaum- Sternberger Foundation http://tsfoundation.com/aboutus.cfm
Value Added Mausoleum http://www.mausoleum.com/whybuild.htm

INDEX

A

Alamance County Courthouse, 233
Albert Einstein, 190
Alfano, 35, 36, 37, 38, 39, 40, 72
Alleghany County, 239
Almanace County Courthouse, 50
Andy Griffith, iii
Ararat River, 23, 173
Arlington Memorial Bridge, iv
Arlington National Bridge, 171
Armfield, 98

B

Banner, 148, 149
Barre, Vermont, 34
BB & T Bank, 249
Bethabara, iii
Bienenstock, 154
Blue Ridge, iii, 22, 23, 28, 245, 246, 247
Booth Brothers, 166, 167
Bowman Gray, 187, 188
Brower Mill Bridge, 173
Brower Mill Granite Bridge, 173
Bryn Mawr Avenue Bridge, 172

C

C. Freeman (Diamond Pete) Neese, 170
Cape Fear and the Yadkin Valley Railroad, 21
Cape Fear and Yadkin Valley Railroad, e, 24, 53
Central United Methodist Church, 120
CF & YV Railway, 29
Charles Myers, 155
Chiddingstone Kent, England, 11
Christopher Binder, 267
Col. Francis Fries, 79, 80
Curbing, 7

D

D'Amico, 42, 43
Daniel Boone, 193
Daniel Humphries, 11
Detroit, Michigan, 31, 89, 198
Dietrich, 1, 2, 269
Dodge Brothers, 31, 89, 90, 91
Donald R. Shelton, 267
Dr. Arthur Gates, 180
Dr. Ashby, 60
Dr. Henry H. Kapp, 159
Dr. Laurimer Jennings (L.J.) Moorefield, Sr., 58
Dr. Moir Martin, 63, 65
Dr. Roy C. Mitchell, 61
Durham, 194

E

E. W. Myers, 151
Emeterio, 43
Episcopal Church of the Holy Comforter, 118

F

Fawcett, 65, 129, 130, 149
First Baptist Church, 12, 50, 85, 89, 106, 116, 154, 202, 203
First National Bank, 68, 129, 130
First Presbyterian, 50, 110
Fisher Park, 141, 142, 148
Flat Rock, iii, 26, 57, 113, 114, 115, 116, 203
Flat Rock Baptist Church, 203
Fort Fisher, 197
Fort Knox, iv, 255
Four Freedoms Park, e, 259, 270
Frank A. Weston, 47, 125
Franklin D. Roosevelt, 260
Fries Manufacturing Company, 81

G

Galloway, 50, 138, 139
General Greene, 211, 213, 227
Governor Montague, 168
Grace Moravian Church, 115

Granite City, iii, 26
Granite Lodge No. 322, 50
Grayson, 133, 134, 154, 155, 156
Green Hill, 12
Green Hill Cemetery, e, iii, 14, 15, 141, 199, 200, 202, 203, 213, 247, 270
Greensboro Country Club, 149
Greensboro, N.C., 28
Guilford County Courthouse, 49, 50, 234
Guilford Courthouse Battleground, 211

H

Hadley, 126, 249
Harry Barton, e, 47, 48, 49, 50, 125, 133, 138, 234, 235, 238
Hearp, 162
Herman Stone, 17, 18
Herman Stone Company, 17
Holcomb Hardware, 70, 134
Holy Angels Catholic Church, 42, 53, 117

I

Immanuel Lutheran College, 252
Immanuel Luthern College, 252
Italy, 34, 42

J

J. W. Fry, 28
J.E. Kirkman, 186
Jack Sargent, iii, 31, 32, 79, 107, 127, 132, 205, 267
Jefferson Standard Insurance, 247
John Davis, e, 31, 32
John Hemenway Duncan, 94
John Lindsay, 259
John Prather Frank, 132, 180
Judge David Schenck, 211
Julius A. Gray, 28

K

Kahn, 259
Keesee, 84, 85, 86, 87, 88, 89, 267, 269
Keren Happuch Turner, 224

Kiwanis, 63, 64, 65
Kochtitzky, 182

L

Lacy S. Vernon, 267
Lancaster, PA, 120, 198
Latham, 141, 147, 148
Laurel Bluff Cotton Mills, 23

M

Main Street, Mount Airy, 32, 69, 107, 108, 109, 110, 127, 129
Manhattan, 94, 259
Martin Memorial Hospital, 58, 60, 61, 62, 64, 65
Martinsville, 84, 85, 86, 87, 88, 89, 196, 243, 269
mausoleum, 31, 77, 78, 79, 80, 83, 89, 92, 94, 98, 100, 101, 270
Mayberry, iii
Mitchell, 65, 66, 134, 207, 259
Moorefield Eye, Ear, Nose, and Throat Hospital, 58, 59
Moravian, 11, 53, 81, 82, 115
mouldings, 33
Mount Airy Friends, 109
Mount Airy Granite, c, e, i, iii, 1, 4, 12, 13, 14, 16, 17, 26, 27, 31, 33, 48, 49, 50, 65, 79, 80, 84, 87, 88, 105, 106, 108, 110, 116, 117, 120, 125, 141, 143, 146, 154, 164, 170, 171, 172, 173, 175, 179, 185, 187, 190, 191, 193, 199, 200, 202, 205, 206, 210, 211, 216, 218, 230, 233, 234, 235, 237, 242, 243, 245, 246, 253, 255, 257
Mount Airy Museum of Regional History, ii, 35, 38, 39
Mount Airy Post Office, 72, 74

N

National Register of Historic Places, 126, 127, 154, 233, 248
NC State Bell Tower
　　North Carolina State, e, 208, 209
New Hanover County Courthouse, 241
North Carolina Granite Corporation, iv, v, 1, 16, 17, 26, 31, 35, 42, 58, 77, 79, 80, 113, 127, 132, 199, 267, 270
North State Improvement Company, 22

O

Oak Ridge, 225
Oak Ridge Military Acadamy, 277

Oakdale Cemetery, iii, 31, 32, 40, 42, 43, 60, 79, 135, 149, 179, 180, 181, 182
Oakwood Cemetery, 78, 85, 92, 98, 187

P

Penn, 101, 103, 223, 259
Peoples Bank, 84
Peter Booth, 165, 167
Peter Francisco, 219
Philadelphia, 28, 47, 122, 123, 124, 125, 148, 172, 256
Piedmont and Mount Airy Division, 23
Pilot Life Insurance, 50, 249
Presbyterian, 47, 50, 105, 110, 111, 113, 114, 200, 270

Q

Q.E.P.D, 43

R

railroad, iii, 21, 23, 26, 34, 53, 81, 151, 200, 256, 267
Randolph County Courthouse, 242
Rectory of Holy Child Roman Catholic Church, 123
Reeves Community Center, 60, 62, 65, 66
Reynolds, 81, 187, 188, 221
Richmond and Danville Railroad, 21, 212
Riverside Drive, 27
Roach, 100, 150, 151, 153, 164, 200, 202
Roanoke, Virginia, 81
Robert Berks, 190
Robert Browne, 267
Robert Ferris, 267
Rotary Club, 58, 87, 132, 157, 248, 269
Ruritan, 57

S

Salem, iii, 7, 8, 9, 23, 61, 62, 66, 78, 79, 80, 81, 82, 83, 84, 143, 159, 187, 188, 218, 224, 245, 248, 269
Sam Hennis, 133
Samuel Henry Kress, 229
Scalpellini, 34
Schenck, 220
Schlosser, 145

Scotland, 110, 141
Shaffner, 79, 80, 84, 89, 159, 267
Southeastern Railway, 63
Southern Chair Company, 186
Springthorpe, 131
St. Charles Borromeo Seminary Group, 124
St. Margaret's Roman Catholic Church, 120
Stephen M. Hale, 65, 133, 135
Stone Cutters Union, 44, 45
stonecutter, 11
Stonecutters, e, 33, 34, 58
Stuart, 23, 61, 108
Surry County Courthouse, 50, 235, 236, 237, 238
Surry County Historical Society, i
Surry County Historical Society Minick Collection, v, 4, 24, 26, 105, 112
Sylvania Mausoleuam, 93

T

Terry Sanford, 154
Tesh, e, 53, 54, 55, 108
Thomas Woodroffe, 12
Tomlinson, 50
Trenton Battle Monument, 178
Trevathan, 183
Trinity Episcopal, 53, 108, 203

U

U.S. Department of Agriculture, 251
U.S. Grant, 95
Ulysses S. Grant, 94, 97, 202
UNCG, 50, 51
Union Trust Building, 253
United States Bullion, 255

V

Vahalla Mausoleum, 92
Vestibule Design, 77, 78

W

W. D. Rowe, 150, 151

W. J. Byeryly, 67
Wachovia, 11, 79, 81, 82, 187
Wanamaker, 256
William Hooper, 222, 223
William S. Martin, 267
Wilmington, 28, 53, 150, 200, 202, 223, 240, 241, 270
Wineskie, 157
Woodroffe, iii, 11, 13, 14, 15, 16, 21, 26, 31, 53, 79, 106, 202, 203, 267
World War II, 191, 229
Wright Brothers, iv, 175, 176, 177, 270
Wright Brothers Memorial, iv

Z

Zion Baptist Church, 111, 112
Zion Reformed Church, 121

Former well gazebo located on the campus of Oak Ridge Military Acadamy.

This gazebo is dedictated to Professor John Allen Holt, former principle and his brother, Martin Hicks Holt by their brother Robert Oascar Holt.

(ORMA web page)

Made in the USA
Columbia, SC
04 October 2024